IT'S
TIME

The Journey to Restore Man's Love

VALLI M.
PERKINS

WESTBOW
PRESS®
A DIVISION OF THOMAS NELSON
& ZONDERVAN

WestBow Press books may be ordered through booksellers or by contacting:

WestBow Press
A Division of Thomas Nelson & Zondervan
1663 Liberty Drive
Bloomington, IN 47403
www.westbowpress.com
1 (866) 928-1240

ISBN: 978-1-5127-2999-3 (sc)
ISBN: 978-1-5127-3000-5 (hc)
ISBN: 978-1-5127-3001-2 (e)

Library of Congress Control Number: 2016901881

Print information available on the last page.

WestBow Press rev. date: 6/10/2016

For those wanting use of their eyes

*"Then the eyes of the blind shall be opened, and
the ears of the deaf shall be unstopped."*

– Isaiah 35:5

CONTENTS

PREFACE

"In the beginning God created the heaven and the earth....
²⁶And God said, Let us make man in our image, after our
likeness: and let them have dominion over the fish of the sea,
and over the fowl of the air, and over the cattle, and over all
the earth, and over every creeping thing that creepeth upon
the earth. ²⁷So God created man in his own image, in the
image of God created he him; male and female created he
them" (Genesis 1:1, 26, 27).

The first chapter of Genesis contains a visual rendering of our reigning Father, His power, and the beginning of His wonderful creations. What begins to unfold is the wonderful plan of a life complete in a perfect environment that He had envisioned for man. God's plan was created from a concealed time that had neither beginning nor end, which masterfully gave man life—a divine position, authority, and domain, to embody a life of a holy priesthood in the image in which he was created.

The beginning of the world and the creation of man has always been an explorative element of mankind's discussions. Many of these discussions become entangled in unfamiliar or mysterious territory, generating a conglomerate of theories, philosophies, and interpretations. It has only been in recent years that a number of noted scholars acknowledged that many of the written texts and compositions regarding the beginning were not based on fact; rather, they were actually hypotheses and theoretical science. Man and the beginning has been speculated, imagined, and even calculated. However, the question begs to be both asked and answered:

has man ever given thought to seek truth? Not the truth that is based on our knowledge or interpretation, but the truth that is revealed and made known only through the Holy Spirit of God. The vision and mysteries of God cannot be explored or understood through man's intellect or knowledge. Only through God's Word and His Spirit are these truths spiritually revealed or discerned (cf. 1 Corinthians 2:9, 10; 12-14). Many skeptics who have analyzed the Bible have decided its transcripts are mere fables or, at best, inspirational writings. However, no person will ever see the Scriptures as God's inspired Word if he has not believed and has not invited the guidance of the Holy Spirit to direct him towards truth.

Some of God's Word was written in a simplistic form, making it easy to understand. Other areas of Scripture were written in God's hidden wisdom and remain a mystery to those with unbelieving hearts and minds. While man may be at different levels of growth in his study of God's Word, the Holy Spirit comes to give an understanding to all who seek Him. Scripture is a revelation of this very truth. Faithful reading of God's Word places the student of the Bible in continuous presence before Him, reverencing, seeking and building trust for a lasting relationship with his truest friend, the Heavenly Father. Believing in this relationship allows God's treasures and mysteries in Scripture to be unveiled so greatly in a believer's understanding, that it is seen as clear as a vision.

How do we build that kind of connection and relationship with God? Simple! We do so with belief, by surrendering our whole self and recognizing the one true and living God. He is the Creator of the universe, of all life and the God of man's salvation. Man's belief in this truth is an open invitation for God to rule and reign within him. It's this spiritual position and reverence that creates man's marvelous connection.

In man's beginning in the garden of Eden when Adam stood in one accord with his Father, God gave him dominion to fulfill and rule all living things on the earth. God also gave Adam authority to *call*, i.e., name all of His creatures, and the names were honored (cf. Genesis 2:19, 20).

However, man lost that connection as a result of sin, ultimately causing his intended position to be spiritually concealed as his penalty. Adam was positioned to govern the earth by fulfilling the acts of righteousness and understanding life, people, and nature. However, Adam fell into rebellion against his Father through disobedience, and shame drove him to hide. Little did he know, not only was he not hidden from God, but these actions would dictate the same results in his future—hiding and covering his sinful acts. Adam's lost love concealed his destiny, and the results further penetrate the heart of God even today, when man's continuous sins are hidden or ignored.

If only we could comprehend what still pulls at our heartstrings when we step outside of God's will in disobedience. Our Heavenly Father's loving Spirit arouses our consciousness to our sin. In times of trouble, man's spirit almost spontaneously calls out, "My God," or, "Lord, have mercy!" Why is this? Because even when we still question or doubt God, the Spirit within knows and still acknowledges the *One* who is in control. Even the worst of criminals with the slightest bit of remorse can experience this consciousness. *This* connection should help us realize something greater in this universe lives on the inside, and carries the mind to a higher level of spiritual knowledge and awareness—if only for a fleeting second! However, man limits himself through sin, causing blindness to his spiritual sight and mind (his spiritual understanding).

But why is *Man* the focus? He was God's first human creation. He was to reflect the image and glory of God in the earth (cf. Genesis 1:26, 27; 5:1; 9:6 and I Corinthians 11:7). Yet sin not only cost him spiritual sight, but waywardness blinded his view of God's marvelous image and glory. Man's reliance is in himself and his abilities, building recognition, and gaining successes and riches of this world. God's earth was never given to man so that its wealth could make him ruler and possessor. Rather, man's righteousness, image and glory were to have dominion; an internal Light that offers truth to spiritual treasures of living holy. When guided by truth, it will be visible to man that the wealth and treasures of this universe are found in LOVE, which comes for the good of the earth and the harmony of humanity. Love prepares the way for a spiritual purpose. God's riches do not encompass money, cars, titles, or other means that speak of success. His inherent gifts are found when seeking a higher spiritual existence. Man must seek to be restored to this position in order to serve in God's *priesthood*—surrendering to His commandments, reverencing and building a spiritual house (himself) made ready for holy works. Conversely, God's priesthood recognizes that man must seek everything in the heavenlies to reclaim a spiritual heritage.

When Man is responsible to live in God's image, he is restored back to the Father's original position. This book will reveal the heart of God toward man through His divine plan. Man must see the benefits of being before God's presence and adhering to His commandments. His understanding and living in this holy *way* aligns the Father's life plan for he and the earth. Trust and believe in Him; the rest is in His hands. Through the Father's plan, man will possess the true ruling (natural and spiritual) that was intended for him on the earth. Our Heavenly Father desires man's humble beginning as created in the garden of Eden. He yearns for his return through Love, Obedience, and Communion (L.O.C), the spiritual access to the treasures of God.

CHAPTER ONE
GOD'S IMAGINATION ABANDONED

In the beginning and before the entrance of sin, *man* (Adam) knew God's voice. He had an attentive ear to hear his Father, submitted to His commandments and became one with Him in spirit. However, when Adam abandoned God's imagination (God's thought and plan) through sin, the dynamics were altered for man's future destinies.

Since the entrance of man's sin, it has blinded him from acknowledging or even recognizing that he possesses an inner man or a spiritual image. His ears have dulled to God's voice—an unknown resonance, so foreign that it is completely unfamiliar. Our Heavenly Father is the connection to the spiritual dwelling within and is the answer to all spiritual directives for man's purpose. For this reason, the Holy Spirit needs to possess His reign in man so that His presence can be known. His Word says that He *is* the *way*, the *truth*, and the *life*, and without a doubt, man must believe that statement. Only then will he have understood God's awesome imagination for him, when he willingly chose to abandon it in the garden of Eden. *"God is a Spirit..."* (John 4:24). Therefore, recognition of Him means to *"...worship him in spirit and in truth."* Man's daily life is comprised of repeatedly nurturing the things concerning his flesh, e.g., talents, intellect, pleasure, health—all of which God has given him. The question is: does man even once think of the importance of building up and maturing the *spirit man* that lives within?

Many have not understood that the *true being* of man's existence *is* his spirit. What happened to conceal the knowledge of his true identity? Who or what is preventing him from knowing the truth and why? Why did it cost man his spiritual understanding and then send him spiraling into isolation, leaving him shackled to perpetual blindness? The answer is older than the ancient of times. He has an adversary whose sole purpose is to drive a wedge between man and God, His truth, and the marvelous plan set for man.

If we could visit the beginning in the early creation, we might be able to imagine God's awesome plan—the plan of having all mankind living and moving in Him. Mankind would have supreme knowledge, abilities, and authorities, all the while existing as worshipping spirit beings. The plan must have been awesome. Even now through our obedience to Him, God's wonderful and marvelous demonstrations of goodness toward mankind are evidence that His faithfulness surpasses our understanding and cannot be measured or explained. How much more would lives have benefited had man continued in his submission to the Father! God wanted a love relationship that would progress to man's perfection (Matthew 5:48). To understand where man has arrived today, we must view his relationship to God from the beginning. So let's unlock and unveil the first treasure that was lost in the garden—*love*.

CHAPTER TWO

MAN LOST HIS FIRST LOVE

*M*any times our passions are formulated from a thought or simply imagining a concept. A true passion is not only imagined, but created to become a reality. The Lord says in Isaiah 55:8, *"For my thoughts are not your thoughts, neither are your ways my ways, saith the LORD."* I am sure God's thought for imagining a loving earthly being created Adam. And out of that same love, God provided everything that was needed to mature Adam in a place for his acts and duties of holiness—becoming that image of light, while submitting to the labors of the *priesthood* of God's perfect garden. Simultaneously, out of love for his Father, Adam *also* succumbed to the image of his Father's ways, clothing his character in humility, righteousness, and holiness.

Adam resided in Eden, a spiritual ecosystem where God's glory and holiness was experienced firsthand, becoming a witness of His constant splendor. He lived among trees that blew at the moving of God's Spirit, birds that nestled in their branches and soared out in assurance, and waters misted upward to nourish the whole earth. The sea knew its place and honored the shores, and the greater and lesser lights glowed at their appointed times. All creation moved in obedience to the rule of the Almighty Master.

God gave Adam proclamation to decree the names of all that He brought before him, and He gave man free reign of his surroundings with only a single omission. This paradise provided shelter, food, and protection—all created from the unconditional love only a Father can reserve for His Son. In a spiritual view, in this paradise the Father provided time, love and care—much like any caretaker would tend and grow his garden, except this growth was a spiritual maturity in His earthly son. He was simply given a garden of *perfection*.

God's molding Adam for this position included the bearing of responsibility, i.e., his given authority to rule and guide through God's righteousness and holiness in the earth. Adam's calling was a duty of service to care for and nurture his surroundings with the abilities that God skillfully perfected in him. God not only created man to worship but also structured his body to offer his service by instilling within him the knowledge of labor and instruction on how to care for God's earthly creations. A certain physical build and stamina would be required to fulfill these rigorous, but gratifying duties—working the grounds of the garden of paradise as a form of worship and honor to his Heavenly Father (Genesis 2:5, 15). Most of all, God desired a relationship that would perfect Adam's *love*—to possess a love for Him as his Father and to revere Him as his God.

If we could look more closely at this beautiful haven created for Adam, we would see that the garden was really a type of ministering ground—a place where God would grow and mature His son's knowledge and spiritual understanding through his submission. Where man's experience of worship was gloriously magnified, and where true reverence was given to his Creator and Father. Eden was a place where Adam was totally exposed before his Father—without any reservations, distrust or doubt, love was shared from a pure and grateful heart. Love was the first *key* to this pure relationship.

However, despite Adam's personal relationship with God, this love was lost. Convinced he could govern and make his own decisions, Adam chose to turn his devotion and dependency away from his Father. It's one of the enemy's subtle deceptions—instilling belief that you can manage without God. I can just hear Adam justifying his action, *"If I'm given authority and knowledge to manage in this dominion, I can certainly live and make my own decisions."* But how do you live and how do you honor God? Not by living outside or ignoring His will. Denying self is one of the beginning steps toward true honor and worship to God. It acknowledges that when the total spirit is submitted to the Father, you trust to release and depend on Him. It releases man of owning the frustration of the mental turbines of life, where he attempts to live his way and call it "living in God's righteousness." That's like viewing a headband versus God's spiritual crown—no comparison! When man's life is draped in holiness, God's truth can begin to break binding strongholds and fettered minds. This is a godly position, which recognizes that true guidance, is a total dependency on God—dispelling any of man's ideals or traditions to make spiritual holiness possible.

Any man who seeks to revere the Jehovah God of Scripture and desire to follow in His holiness is accepting this position of priesthood. He recognizes the Creator as the head of his life, and as mentioned, completely trusting Him to relinquish himself through total surrender and dependence. Consequently, the child of God must learn to deny self and his *own desires*. This type of denying will not neglect; rather, this denial will resist seeking that which gains him the world's recognitions and the approval of man instead of the approval of God. In God's eyes, the flesh is a serviceable tool only! Man was created to serve, and God prefers man's service with a surrendered heart and a righteous spirit. Following God is the only way to genuinely serve Him.

In this earthly realm, man was created to build sincere relationships. What better way to build them than to serve one another! Man has been gifted with talents and/or knowledge that, with time, can be molded into skill sets concentrated for a specific work. However, through spiritual maturity, these same skills can also be activated for the provision of community and for seasons of God's spiritual work and purposes.

To live for God and to be used for His service is a powerful reason for mankind's existence. If only man could realize this truth! He would see the importance of surrendering to one of God's initial priestly callings, i.e., service. In this calling, the child of God reverences His Father and is a servant to others. We are here to serve, serve, serve—to serve a Servant with our service!

Surrender to God's Authority

A man's position of priesthood acknowledges that his strength and power is not his own, but a force from God which enables him through reverence. Being reverent is not a reflection of one's being weak or powerless. On the contrary, reverence recognizes that one is never strong in his own power and ability. Only through God comes strength; He alone is the force, which holds all power and is ready to strengthen believers in times of weakness. The Holy Scriptures states, "...*my strength is made perfect in weakness*" (2 Corinthians 12:9). When man surrenders to this position of dependence or weakness, God guides his every step and can perform amazing works. Acknowledging that weakness and relinquishing control takes maturity and a realization that our greatest strength is to first recognize that we have none—not without the ability of the One who created and ultimately controls all strength.

Remember, "*In all thy ways acknowledge him, and he shall direct thy paths*" (Proverbs 3:6). Not acknowledging the One who is strength inevitably alters the path that has already been prepared for us. God's journey for our life path becomes invisible without transforming the mind to recognize His spiritual force at work in all matters—both natural and spiritual. Man must assume this *surrendering*—embracing a responsibility of posturing oneself in readiness and being available to answer when He calls. Through this positioning, God can bless through His many manifestations.

Surrender inhabits another position of recognition, which is praise. The greatest blessing that can be offered to God comes when man's true glory and blessings are recognized through his thanksgiving. Too many times man easily receives the accolades that belong to others and glory in his own abilities. To give back the glory to Whom it is due is one of the greatest of reverences—displaying not only adoration to God, but also a demonstration of dependency and trust in the Father that He truly is. Building this kind of relationship between man and God takes maturity and is not impossible. Man's remembering that nothing is impossible with Him brings encouragement. *"...With men this is impossible; but with God all things are possible"* (Matthew 19:26). Therefore, man's authority must not be sought; rather, submit to a spiritual authority whose rulings are always righteous and true. Our Heavenly Father is Spirit, and every man possesses that same Spirit! Submit it to God's authority and allow Him to guide you to the strait (*complete*) pathway.

How do you know the Holy Spirit of God is guiding you? That quiet, but familiar voice can always be found in a sincere or answered prayer, in a whisper that causes you to make a crucial change, in an unexpected blessing or in an opened door. Recognize that He is the guide to all men whose hearts are opened to Him. He is always there for those who will submit to His call!

Scripture says that *spirit* knows *spirit*, but again man must seek to unveil his own spirit—that *spirit man* which lives within; it's a spirit which seeks to connect to a higher power. But, instead of man growing spiritually, sin has caused him to lose sight that this spirituality exists. Hence, he struggles to find his way through darkness—a constant frustration that seemingly beats against air with no direction, when all that's required is a surrendered heart to God and His truth. Reading the Word with the aid of the Holy Spirit will allow the reader to view instances when God spoke to an individual's spirit and was heard. Those with surrendered hearts were guided to understand not only His truth but many times His purpose. Prayer is the means to ask for God's guidance in unveiling His truth through spiritual understanding. For those who desire to know Him with a pure heart do not despair—in time, the *understanding* of His Word and way *will* come. This promise has been offered to all mankind through God's Teacher and Comforter—the *Holy Spirit* (cf. Jeremiah 29:13; Matthew 7:7).

Serving God as a priest requires not only love and commitment, but also the understanding that worldly endeavors or advancements are not the precedence when one is building for the kingdom. Certainly, money is necessary to supply basic human needs along the journey. However, when man surrenders to follow God's missions, His miracles supply the provisions. Again, transforming the mind to understand spiritual moves is pivotal to creating the connection and oneness with God. His movements are always for the success of His purpose, not our own. Scripture continually demonstrates that when mankind does not follow God's instructions, his own leading misguides him; hence, God's intended path begins to alter. It is His purpose that has destiny and not meant to be changed, delayed, or halted! Surrendering to His authority and being directed His way pleases Him and grows the believer's relationship with God.

A life that surrenders to God's purposes, functions in His spiritual power and applications. God's sole purpose for man is to live in holiness, direct him toward righteousness and to fulfill His spiritual destinies. Man can only please God when he is led to operate in the Spirit (spiritual thoughts and actions as in Colossians 3:2) with a pure heart. Otherwise, he is led by his own desires and driven to win the affections of others. "*So then they that are in the flesh cannot please God*" (Romans 8:8).

Love seizes the heart of God. It is written that to love God, mankind must keep His commandments to love one another. There is no denying that God's love sustains our daily life; that reason alone should drive man to surrender to God and deny the sin nature of his flesh. It is man's (and mankind) love and devotion for which God yearns. He desires a love of your "whole" heart because only then will you surrender all to him. It's your total surrender to God that creates miracles—and without the rebellion of man's flesh, God can accomplish the works intended for mankind and the earth. Again, God's image is in man, and he has been given ordained authority in the earth for a purpose. However, though man is created in His likeness, it is man's love, salvation and belief in Jesus Christ, which makes him an heir in God's family. Know that you were created in God's love; allow it to reflect in the confidence of who you are. If man is an heir and has been given the authority, he need have no fear in approaching his Heavenly Father. Man should feel privileged to go before Him in all matters of his existence because the realization is that he *came* through his earthly father, but he will *live* through his heavenly Father.

CHAPTER THREE

MAN'S DISCERNMENT LOST THROUGH DECEPTIONS

This chapter will address how the Adversary's lies, schemes, and devices might cause one to be sidetracked from entering a form of priesthood as it did in the Genesis account, the beginning of our world.

Satan has known since the beginning that he must place a wedge between man and God because of the ordained authority man was given through God. Satan is called the prince of this world but Man's given authority is greater if only he understood whose spirit abides within. If man realized that he was created to reflect this awesome *image*, and what that possesses, he would no longer be blind; his way will be *illuminated*, and his *work set free*. However, the Adversary's attacks of deception exist; and his assaults can only be identified with the help of a spiritually transformed mind. Deceptions and lies are an integral part of today's society where various forms of deceit are present—so man must be aware to "acknowledge (that it's real), recognize (identify it), and deny (deprive it) to its destruction." As a believer, we ask for God's help to give us authority and power to avoid this in ourselves and to discern these approaches from others. But in blindness, that authority is not enforced and these approaches are hidden— and one would simply accept that he had no power.

The Word exposes the subtlety and craftiness of the Adversary's deeds, as well as the seemingly unassuming ways in which he attacks. Satan has been twisting God's words into lies or half-truths since the beginning. And when God's spiritual *truths* aren't recognized, Satan's lies and deceptions are viewed as truth! Eve was aware not to eat or touch the forbidden fruit *"lest ye die."* However, Satan caused Eve to doubt what she had heard. *"Yea, hath God said, Ye shall not eat of every tree of the garden?"* Satan's subtle question in Genesis 3:1 was the entry of his deception to Eve, twisting what God had commanded! Satan not only knew that death would be the penalty, but he also knew the *timing* of the penalty: *"And the serpent said unto the woman, Ye shall not surely die: ⁵For God doth know that in the <u>day</u> ye eat thereof, then your eyes shall be opened..."* (Genesis 3:4, 5). Satan knew that if he could grasp her mind to hear, then her flesh would follow the act of rebellion against God as he once did, and they would lose *spiritual* enlightenment. Their minds would be independent of God's, which would reduce Adam and Eve from spiritual to *natural* thinking.

Satan's illusion of death only alluded to earthly and temporal outcomes when he uttered, *"Ye shall not surely die"*—it did not speak to the spiritual ramifications of his deceptive promise. His subtle lie simply hid the whole truth. God is Spirit, and He always speaks from a spiritual perspective. Satan's statements will offer only empty and worldly promises—an immediate form of gratification or an attractive life that can be claimed temporarily. His promise to Eve that she and Adam *would not surely die* was an absolute untruth. This death was twofold and a greater penalty than either of them could have ever imagined. The first death would involve a spiritual separation from God, an end to a time when they normally communed and daily walked in His presence throughout this perfect paradise. That loving fellowship they enjoyed would no longer exist! The second death would be the ultimate penalty—the physical death, the result of waning years of growing old and the body's breaking down under life's physical labors, stresses, and diseases until death.

Can you see how Satan can twist truth to throw the mind into confusion or doubt? Do you see how the tactics of deception can cause you to alter or question your thinking? If God had directly commanded you, would you have been able to hear or discern the differences when the Enemy approached with veiled promises? Would your love have remained devoted? Who would *you* have believed?

In addition to knowing Satan's tactics, man must be truthful in holiness to uphold the position of God's holy priesthood. This is another of Satan's attempts to discredit God's truth and ability—placing doubt to divert the believer's mission and holy stance. Therefore, man's spiritual identification must reflect a walk that continuously represents who God is; HOLY. *"...Be ye holy; for I am holy"* (1 Peter 1:16; cf. Leviticus 19:2). Satan's attacks are ongoing and never yielding, but the believer must realize that he doesn't have a way to attack strategically unless the ways are shown to him! He is considered the prince of this world, but unlike God, who is *omniscient* (all-knowing), *omnipotent* (almighty), or *omnipresent* (universal, ever-present). He can only attack that which we activate through our *words* and *deeds*.

Satan takes every negative word spoken or every wrong deed performed and uses it as a tool of destruction. He will continually attack the mind, reminding the man of failures and past mistakes, or he will keep the mentality in a state of confusion regarding current circumstances or belief. And he will continue to attack the body where it is weak—offering in excess, in obsessions, to improper visuals, or invitations to satisfy an appetite. The Scripture states that man must *"Put on the whole armour of God, that ye may be able to stand against the wiles of the devil"* (Ephesians 6:11). This verse addresses the importance of transforming the mind to live in God's holiness, which opens and renews man's understanding and discernment about what goes on around him *spiritually*. Even though we live in this natural realm called earth, we are surrounded by another real and very active world that is spiritual. This spiritual world consists of God's heavenly angels (or messengers) who help us, but evil principalities also that work against God's missions. Sadly, many times these evil principalities act through mankind! However, when God's truth lives within, we are confident in whom we follow. His Word reminds us to be assured, to stand bold and not to be deceived. We are the joint heirs of Christ, and there will be no mistaking the wisdom of God's mission. His Word says, *"If ye then be risen with Christ, seek those things which are above, where Christ sitteth on the right hand of God. Set your affections on things above, not on things on the earth"* (Colossians 3:1, 2).

Another tactic of the Adversary involves the deception, which causes people to doubt, and questions whether God's ancient chronicles and written records were indeed God-inspired. Our Adversary is a master of raising concerns that individuals may have injected or removed some of the Scripture, thereby changing it's original content or interpretation. As Christians, we must not allow these tactics to cause us to stumble. An issue such as the accuracy of the original Word of God is beyond our control; preservation of the truth is in God's hands. His Word clearly warns of the penalty that awaits those who might change or alter his message, and He will not forget! God is Truth, His Word is truth, and when the Holy Scriptures are applied in our lives, we can clearly see evidence that His words are spiritually *alive* with power and purpose.

Other skeptics have intellectualized that what the pens of ready writers have recorded are merely inspirational messages. They erroneously surmise that God's effectual works or His miracles are attributable to a person's good fortune, gifts, and talents. Who willed the good fortune or gave the gifts or talents? Some think the Spirit of God cannot dwell in man. Still others who might possess spiritual knowledge but do not always have spiritual understanding—not believing God's treasures and riches are available to all mankind. God is *truth*, and His order of life is the same throughout the universe. If we are His reflection, we should see His Spirit and character at work in us—we can also see the same gifting, talents, reflection, and character in others around the world. Even in a foreign country, people will spiritually recognize a fellow believer because of the immediate connection of spirit and their common understanding. They will extend themselves because they recognize the same spiritual character.

The same can be experienced in lands where the Scripture is unavailable; the true Spirit of God is that *"lively stone"* within—which lives and alters lives and can be felt through the evidences of the Holy Spirit.

Do not be deceived; the true Spirit connects us all. Yet, clearly Adam became disconnected from God by stepping away from his appointed position—the connection to priesthood, a holy position created for man operating in righteous authority. Adam's connection to God for this priesthood had purpose, not only for his path, but also the path of mankind. It was a call to surrender—surrendering his mind, body, soul and will and become obedient to the guidance of God. It was a priestly position of authority, which would call all things on the earth to become subject to him, if he would follow in His Father's ways. This preparation for maturity would come through his: obedience and worship, receiving God's direction, offering perfect sacrifices, following commandments, populating the earth, accepting His guidance for eating, and maintaining the earth. His preparation had great purpose. Yet, the design and plan of God was destroyed by sin through man's selfish pursuit. Satan's craftiness led him to abandon his faithfulness toward God, which negated all spiritual enlightenment. Where insight was a gift given by God to illuminate and guide the thoughts of man, it was now incomprehensible.

Every step away from God and His holy purpose moves mankind into continual darkness. For this reason, the understanding of the position to surrender is pertinent. Surrender is not a position of degradation or to be assumed as less than as some suppose, but a submission to humbleness. This is a *"Trust in my Father"* position, with the responsibility of being *humble* and allowing God to perform His directions for the spirituality of mankind. God wants man to assume this position to gain the ultimate sacrifice of the flesh—his surrender—where love would build a relationship of trust, respect, reverence, and submission to his Father's authority.

A Transformed Mind

Establishing a spiritually transformed mind is crucial. Adam's willingness to surrender his will to God originally built their loving and righteous relationship. It existed without hidden agendas or deception—only liberty, wholeness, and a life in truth. Without this position, man is unable to be directed spiritually toward what God has for his expected end. He must realize, without a doubt, that everything placed within him to achieve greatness for God's kingdom on this earth was already formed within his spirit, knowledge, and biological structure. Man will be able to accomplish everything within God's permissive will if he submits, renews his mind (Romans 12:1, 2; Ephesians 4:23), recognizes the source of his power (Romans 13:1), establishes God's righteous position, and is working toward completing his predestined purpose. As he humbly follows the path that was destined for him, God allows his kingdom work to be illuminated for the world to witness (e.g., Mother Teresa, Nelson Mandela, Mahalia Jackson, Mohandas Gandhi, and many others who have followed the spirit of love and mission). Following His purpose clearly demonstrates that the mission is not about you getting recognition, but the work—surrendering enables the work to flow, brings attention to the needs, all to accomplish a higher purpose and destiny. And know that the spiritual outcome of His destinies outweigh anything that we can fathom or imagine. Therefore, following purpose begins to train and mature man's spirituality, clearly enabling God to effectively enhance man's gifts and present opening doors that will aid in completing God's intentions.

Some men have been called or elected to specific duties tailored exactly for them, while others have been linked to work with others as one body, using the gifts and talents God has given them. Whatever the path, rest assured that all have been purposefully charged to live lives of righteousness by following Christ's example (cf. 1 Peter 2:21). Following Christ is a reflection of maturity. Those who have chosen to be led by the Spirit will find kingdom building is their basis for ministering, edifying, and enlightenment for the glory of God and not for themselves.

The Scripture says, "*Let nothing be done through strife or vainglory; but in lowliness of mind let each esteem other better than themselves. Look not every man on his own things, but every man also on the things of others*" (Philippians 2:3, 4). We all have paths and destinations assigned, but none is greater than acknowledging others in their journey and aiding one another along the way. The mind and transformation that God has imagined for mankind is extending a love toward all. Honoring others is the selfless love (agape) and one of the greatest extensions of God.

When you're called to go forward in His purpose, be persistent to complete that calling. In your submission, God's love will grant you liberty (freedom/authority), covering (protection), provision (open doors), and a divine character (spirituality), all of which perform together for the journey. Do not be deceived into thinking that you may have misunderstood the call or that God made a mistake because your skills aren't adequate. At times we may not understand the calling or why we were chosen, but if we are totally dependent on Him, He will equip us with what is needed to fulfill the task. Eventually, He will give you the understanding of why you were chosen for this particular service. Sadly, some have not been in tune to hear His voice and have ignored or missed a calling, and thereby failing to see Him perform miracles for humanity and the world. All He seeks is a "yes" when He calls. Your agreement means that you are available, responsible, and accountable. Rest in your faith and assurance to trust Him!

Two Forms of Priesthood

All men have been called to live as an example of Christ on the earth. Living a life that models Christ is to stand upright with God before families, neighbors, acquaintances, and friends, to follow His way. Submitting to His way is a type of priesthood in that you surrender to God's commandments and follow the passions He has gifted in your heart. Your gift could be a passion such as repairing homes for the elderly, coaching the youth, or giving aid from your field of expertise to the underserved. Whatever the journey, it was given as a passion that will fulfill God's priestly mission of service to humanity.

God has also called certain men to live lives that are sanctified, holy, and set apart for a sacred service. Identified and positioned by God to guide the church, these men have been *called* to be a priest (pastor). Their lives are impacted by God's calling, keeping them spiritually guided in ways for ministering to all mankind. God expects His priest to be an extension of His message for growing the church's belief and faith in Jesus Christ through the Word. Where God's Word is certainly used to admonish evil, a priest knows that God's Word also washes mankind clean by teaching of God's goodness, mercies and the Way, which leads to eternal life. His heart is not quick to judge by the Word; rather, he offers a righteous and just example that teaches God's blessing through the Word. The priest (pastor) is on a continued path and journey to serve mankind and to edify the family of God. His rewards consist of all that God promises to those who choose to live in His light—spiritual riches and treasures of love, holy and righteous living, forgiveness, contentment, and expectations of the eternal blessings and promises of God. Ultimately, a priest is a teacher of God's light, especially for those whose lives have been shadowed by darkness—for those children who have lost their way and need guidance through the faithfulness of His Word. The little ones in Christ (young in years or young spiritually) may need time to be taught their belief and led to grow in Him, as he continues to guide them toward God's truth. Without a shepherd to guide, how do they believe, feel or hear the heart of God toward them? God's Word tells us *"How then shall they call on him in whom they have not believed? and how shall they believe in him of whom they have not heard? and how shall they hear without a preacher?"* (Romans 10:14). God's truth provides the guided way and a priest's duty as mediator is to follow His way as an example before mankind—leading the misguided to the promises of eternal life and the blessed hope extended to all generations.

In ancient times, only chosen men (high priests) could go before God for the people. Today, believers are under a new covenant in God; the veil in the tabernacle of the holy of holies was torn, and every believer now has the blessed privilege of going before God for himself. At one time, many did not know of His existence or had even heard of His name. Therefore, let's understand how one such purpose came into existence and why a priest's calling is so important.

A Priesthood Fulfilled—Why and Who was Called

A correlation exists between man and the position of priesthood; it was given as a position that adhered to righteous authority and duties in the years following the garden. Before sin, God's character in man led him towards righteousness and an obedient Spirit submitted when called for service. This same God is in man's character and can be evident in the church, home and the world; fulfilling a priesthood devoted to God's services, purpose and destinies. But it was very difficult to find such men during the early years of the world when laws were few, and only chosen men knew God.

In the beginning when nations were being formed on the earth, no laws were in place to govern God's people (the Israelites) toward righteous living. Some had no means of hearing or even having the knowledge that God existed. Therefore, to allow His people to know of Him, God appointed and prepared intercessors to bring knowledge and holy declarations to the ears of His people.

Because the Israelites lacked knowledge of Him and the nature of their living spoke to an unholy lifestyle, these chosen intercessors had to be men of godly character who had earned the respect of their people. They entered what was called a priesthood, which meant that they were set apart—not only to submit under God's commandments and bring awareness of Him but also to perform prayers and holy rituals in the temple according to God's instructions. Their willingness to observe and follow the order of God's steps brought them into a position to serve. Can you see the spiritual side to this order? Because His people lacked belief, faith, and knowledge, God delivered His messages through those who did believe and were submissive to His will. From Adam's sin came the penalty of spiritual separation and blindness; from blindness, came a people of unbelief, which cost them the inability to know that a relationship with God was even a possibility!

Therefore, priests and prophets became vital instruments for God during this period. They became especially necessary during the aftermath of the Israelites' exodus from Egypt. During this difficult time, lawlessness ran rampant, and disobedience caused many of the Israelites to lose sight of whose people they were. While enslaved in Egypt, their exposure to foreign practices, rituals, and traditions caused them to adopt a new devotion to strange gods. They began to abandon their fathers' beliefs and the teachings of God. Finding themselves disconnected, they needed to experience for themselves the faith of their fathers. Therefore, because their sin had caused them to stray from hearing, God instituted a method of cleansing through sacrifices and offerings. He raised up high priests to communicate His heart and to bring them to the knowledge of possessing levels of faith that surpass all natural understanding. The *first level of faith*, which had to be established was embracing a belief and a knowledge of God. Who was this deity? The God of Abraham who was first known as God Almighty and then Jehovah or Yahweh!

The Holy Scriptures teach that faith comes by hearing the Word of God (Romans 10:17), and throughout these biblical generations, He called many priests and prophets to receive and deliver His Word to the Israelites as well as to people of other nations. As has been witnessed through the centuries, a person must embrace belief and a changed mind before faith can help him begin a growth toward spiritual maturity. Earlier priests and prophets, such as Noah, Abraham, Moses, and Isaac, all heard God and responded. These obedient followers of the faith chose not to be led by their wisdom and strength, but by the One who knew them best and the path required for the character of His people. Many times the journey of each one of these prophets and priests took alternate routes that were unexpected or even unexplained. However, these patriarchs understood that the One who had planned every step before their birth had masterfully orchestrated their destiny.

As a chosen vessel, man needed only to be available, trusting, and obedient, and possess a willingness to go all the way with God. A man is called to the priesthood when he can be trusted and has become a hearer and a doer of God's will through a life that pleases. God knew that His people had abandoned the ways of their fathers after their exodus from Egypt; they needed to hear how to discard their previous slave mentality and renew a life of righteousness. Over these years sin came without boundaries, and the sacrifices that were once required as an offering would no longer satisfy God. He would need to eventually send to earth the ultimate sacrificial Lamb, the second Adam, priest and chief Shepherd to the world, Jesus Christ, through the physical body of His Son. Few understood that an all-powerful God only wanted man to gain back what he had originally lost in the garden—his spiritual relationship and understanding. Both could be obtained again through embracing His commandments (cf. John 14:15, 21).

The *second level of faith* was not simply acquiring the knowledge of God in Word but also having an experience and becoming eyewitnesses to the Word through the human form of God's Son, Jesus Christ. His Son would be the evidence and testimony to many that God existed—and exists today—by becoming a living witness of God's truth.

> *"Jesus answered them, I told you, and ye believed not: the works that I do in my Father's name, they bear witness of me; [30]I and my Father are one. [38]But if I do, though ye believe not me, believe the works: that ye may know, and believe, that the Father is in me, and I in him"* (John 10:25, 30, 38).

As was witnessed in the flesh, He is a true, living testimony and example of His Father's way, truth, and life—a life that would demonstrate the truth that even when living a life of holiness, trials of *perfecting* will come. Many times in life, people may not initially understand God and

His Word, but a laborer for God's purposes drives godly actions; hence, the evidence and the proof that God and the Word lives. Holy living and possessing a spiritually changed mind helps man to see more clearly and become an eyewitness to an invisible God. If His Truth is seized, hearing His Word not only transforms the mind and stimulates action, but hearing opens the visibility of Him all around us. This life is not ours; it belongs to God. Take hold to follow the example of His Son's life and seize the opportunities to witness and labor for Him in boundless ways. Man may not always know the destination, but offering a transformed life to God makes the journey an honor and privilege—and the *calling* always gratifying!

During these years of Christ's ministry, people were also eyewitness to His miracles. Tangible evidences could be examined, spoken to, or even touched to support their belief. Becoming witnesses to His actual miracles made a world of difference for so many who became believers. His physical likeness was that of normal man but a spiritual blueprint of an awesome character of God. Even though He was the Son of God, He was housed in human flesh, making it tangible and common for man to see a possibility of himself. He was physically relatable, lived as a commoner, spoke as they did, but totally committed to His Father's will to be a holy example. He would destroy Satan's attacks by teaching God's truth and demonstrating His perfect love toward adults, children, tradesmen, and all who would be opened to hear. He was the Son of God but was abased, and knew how to converse with all men; visiting with the youth and the commoners and even had discussions with town clergy, physicians and social dignitaries. He was all things to all men throughout his ministry by identifying with humanness, but His truth won souls through hearts of conversion. He was also a teacher to those given to Him (the disciples), preparing them for the time of His departure, and readying them for a work that would reach the world. Regardless of social background, all mankind had access to Him to become eyewitnesses to the existence of holiness.

God proclaimed Jesus Christ a priest forever—a priest made with an oath to possess a better hope for mankind. His oath (or testament) stated, *"By so much was Jesus made a surety of a better testament"* (Hebrews 7:22). *"But now hath he obtained a more excellent ministry by how much also he is the mediator of a better covenant, which was established upon better promises"* (Hebrews 8:6). Because of this oath, Jesus became the Guarantor of a new covenant, which opened the understanding of His love and truth to a better way, a better hope, and a holy priesthood for *all* of God's citizens. His desire is to grow and build man's spiritual house into a holy priesthood, whereby his life would be a reflection of Jesus Christ, and his worship would be a true and spiritual offering unto God.

We indeed need the instructions of priests and pastors of churches to bring new converts to a place of belief and to the guidance of our Lord and Savior Jesus Christ. Yet, whereby earthly priests are assigned by man and may have frailties and die, God's *Priest* (Jesus) has been assigned forever as He lives forever. We can give our petitions to Him, and He will always intercede for us. That's guaranteed! *"Wherefore he is able also to save them to the uttermost that come unto God by him, seeing he ever liveth to make intercession for them"* (Hebrews 7:25). He has been declared the High Priest, and His continual assignment is to show man a better way to draw closer to God.

So why does today's priesthood struggle? Does man appoint the leadership that should be called by God? Are we following God's law or man's? Scripture tells us:

> *"For the law maketh men high priests which have infirmity; but the word of the oath, which was since the law, maketh the Son, who is consecrated for evermore.* [24]*But this man, because he continueth ever, hath an unchangeable priesthood"* (Hebrews 7:28, 24).

Throughout mankind's existence for a couple thousand years, spiritual barriers and unbelief are still being conquered, where man is still being reborn to witness and testify of a true and living God. However, as we've seen since the rebellion in the garden of Eden, generations of lives has suffered—man's faith needed to be restored. First, the world needed *knowledge* that the one true God exist, He lives and His Way is truth. Secondly, mankind became *eyewitnesses* of Him through His Son—a time when believers could view the Word in the flesh and physically see His miracles accomplished through Christ. But today while we have not been privileged to hear the Word from God's ancient priest and prophets nor were we present when the Word came to mankind in flesh, we have been blessed to read through the spiritual chronicles (the Bible) of God. And greater yet, God's love has paved an example of an upright life for mankind to follow through His reverenced Son, Jesus Christ.

God's purpose for recording Christ's life and His lineage on the earth was to serve as a remembrance—a spiritual record of history to be passed on and taught to future generations. That said, a priest's duty, both naturally and spiritually, is to impact our future for the good of this world and to encourage a whole new generation of believers to come even higher! He is now calling mankind to proclaim an even higher level of faith in Him—the *third level of faith*, which trusts and receives *the Holy Spirit*. [The Bible refers to the Holy Spirit as *He* based on the authority and power from which it comes, which also speaks to the authority that was destined for man, had he held his righteous position. However, the Scripture clearly states that God is Spirit, and the Holy Spirit is of God.] *He* (when referenced) is Spirit and a force that cannot be audibly heard, seen or touched, but He is surely the One who can fill us with His presence and power. The Spirit of a holy God promises the believer that He comes with power to do the works of the kingdom. He can only be heard with a pure heart and received through a spiritually surrendered mind. Our ancient generations were given the opportunity to hear His Word and physically become eyewitnesses to His Way. Nonetheless, *It's Time* to possess a transformed mind and to receive the experience of the Holy Spirit's power and authority; *it's time* that man know whose image he is and rise above the things he can see to accomplish it all from a spiritual perspective, "*If ye then be risen with Christ, seek those things which*

are above, where Christ sitteth on the right hand of God." (Colossians 3:1).
The Scripture say *He* is the ultimate Teacher who will reveal all spiritual knowledge and recall it to our remembrance. God's Word says:

> *"But God hath revealed them unto us by his Spirit: for the Spirit searcheth all things, yea, the deep things of God…* [13]*Which things also we speak, not in the words which man's wisdom teacheth, but the Holy Ghost teacheth; comparing spiritual things with spiritual."* (I Corinthians 2:10, 13).

Today, we are blessed to have not experienced many of the spiritual struggles that our forefathers had to endure because of their lack of faith—the rituals, the offerings, and the special sacrifices that were required. Yet, we can read their history and learn from these various circumstances to possibly avoid dire situations. Records bear ancient chronicles of mankind's trials, tribulations, and generations of consequences due to sin, but also note the recorded triumphs as well. They are an enlightenment of the blessed and eternal hope that further grows belief and trust in a God who is victorious! These times were recorded so that no longer do we have to suffer the consequences of these errors, but use them as a stepping-stone to mature man's belief, to help him stand bold in the faith. These accounts could then be passed on to instill holiness in the lives of our future generation.

The struggles of mankind were not restricted to a particular nationality or a certain class of people. Records display examples from countless regions of the earth addressing the rich, the poor, the young, and the old who experienced the various changes of life: unbelief, disobedience, humility, pride, love, and loss. God's grace and mercy is presented daily with the opportunity to change misguided paths. However, as is revealed throughout history, trials are certain to be repeated when God's spirituality is abandoned—that is, if they have not been learned. History's chronicled examples are foundational, and are strength in a spiritual journey to priesthood.

To believe in God is to believe in His Son and to receive the Holy Spirit. When Jesus departed this earth and no longer walked with His disciples, He promised to send them the Holy Spirit as a Comforter, replacing that void of His presence. However, knowing how the hearts of His disciples concerned themselves with the days and times of what was to come, Jesus wanted them to understand that God's *kingdom work* was the focus of importance. The Holy Ghost would come to empower them to accomplish that work. *"But ye shall receive power after that the Holy Ghost is come upon you: and ye shall be witnesses unto me both in Jerusalem, and in all Judea, and in Samaria, and unto the uttermost part of the earth"* (Acts 1:8). We should be the generations of that *third level of faith*, operating and trusting in the teachings and guidance of the Holy Spirit. As it is in the natural, so it is in the spiritual! In the natural Christ was once our physical example on earth, teaching, living and proclaiming the Word of His Father's way. Today He is calling man to reconnect through His created image. He is seeking those to experience Him spiritually through the presence of the Holy Spirit.

Keeping our minds fixed on the things of the kingdom directs our focus to God's ultimate mission and invites the Holy Spirit's presence. It's the way back to a position that Adam possessed with his Father in the beginning—a relationship through a priestly calling.

CHAPTER FOUR

THE FAMILY'S LOSS OF GODLY STRUCTURE

A Godly Headship

How is your relationship with your earthly Father? Well, generally speaking, most children will have great adoration for their fathers or men who are positive role models—they also gravitate towards those who offer them attention or praise from time to time. Children are great imitators of character and men who display a life of authority, strong or confident, the findings are that male children tend to impersonate their role. However at best, children offer their respect to a father figure.

Within a family unit, however, most male children desire to emulate their central authority figure—their father—while growing into adulthood. Yet the rampant immorality in our society and even a tainted family history can lay an undesirable framework for molding a child's character. Some fathers are oftentimes misled into accepting unruly mannerisms and unworthy attributes from their family background as an acceptable foundation for establishing family lifestyles (i.e., "It-worked-for-me-and-I'm-still-here" attitude). These unacceptable foundations can only produce the same damaging characteristics, which ultimately develop an unhealthy relationship between father and child. On the other hand, the man who seeks God has the chance to correct errors in his relationships when he acknowledges the call to become the priest before his family.

A father who has the opportunity to be an example before his children literally has two choices: he can demonstrate a life he has adopted after his earthly father or a life of righteous living from his Heavenly Father. The man who lives a Christ-filled life in the presence of his family will build trust, honor, and respect. Gaining this type of merit from his children is a spiritual move that will reward any father. Fathers need to be open, honest, and revealing, especially regarding their childhood and life mistakes. Not only will this honesty allow children to see that their parents were not perfect people, but mistakes are a natural part of mankind's maturity and God's love exists even in our imperfections. Man can still serve His purpose in life through a repentant heart. This kind of example will grow a generation of honest and righteous individuals who could become leaders and perhaps fathers themselves—thus creating the priest and model that was imagined for man and finally manifested through the example of Jesus Christ—where love and a righteous headship have been perfectly illustrated.

The Natural and Spiritual Family

Where is the beginning of love in a family? In thinking of our first physical *love* experience, we would have to imagine that it must have been an experience felt through our mother's womb (cf. Exodus 13:2, 15; Matthew 1:23, 25). Yes, I'm sure you are saying, "That is not an experience that would have been seared in the minds of most people as a *memory*"; however, I am sure most would agree that a special connection had to exist between a mother and baby during those months in the womb.

In God's great design, the womb of the female was masterfully designed and structured to safely contain and grow an infant's body. That infant is miraculously formed to perfection, while it is held captive to a mother's constant voice, touch, and love. During the transformation of the fetus, the infant is also forming a relationship and awareness. The Scripture tells us that in the beginning of Mary's pregnancy, she traveled to visit her cousin Elisabeth who was also expecting. When Elisabeth heard Mary's greeting and was informed that Mary also was pregnant, the babe in Elisabeth's womb leaped. This illustration seems to indicate that even infants rejoice in the womb and respond to natural stimuli and spiritual experiences!

At birth a child's love is present in an instant, connecting to mother, father and family. Months of caressing and caring for a helpless, but darling, child begin. However, beyond the beginning months of nourishing and nurturing a babe, the father is the one who will eventually set guidelines for growing this child. These guidelines may not immediately encompass physical boundaries, but displaying ways that are good, applying moral standards for a good life and eventually laying a sound foundation for living in spiritual holiness. He not only implements structure and resolve for his family, he also teaches the importance of benevolence beyond the family. Righteousness causes a godly father to look to the heavens as the best illustration of family. With the heavenly congregation as his view, he teaches his family to strive to be harmonious and loving. This type of family exists in the heavens and is proof when we observe verses such as "...Let us make man in our image" (Genesis 1:26). Obviously, this verse does not directly disclose to whom God made this statement; however, His words do express the breadth of oneness and inclusiveness in which they were spoken. All we know is that the Creator represents perfected holiness in *fullness*: "For in him dwelleth all the fulness of the Godhead bodily" (Colossians 2:9). Conversely, whether the statement was directed to the Godhead or to the heavenly host, all exist in His likeness. All are of one perception—a consistent, unchanged family of love. All things are congruent under Him because He is the Creator of all, including the formations of families.

In the beginning God created all living creatures to cohabit the earth in various elements and environments. These numerous breeds and species of families served very different purposes by responding to a calling all their own. Some were made to pollinate, some would grow to hibernate; some creatures not so pleasant to the eye, while others were breathtaking in their beauty. All were uniquely formed, developed and infused with purpose. Every male creature needed a female counterpart to form these families. God's awesome design and purpose was applied to both plant and animals alike. His photosynthetic and biological patterns are plans to fulfill life destinies on this earth. Without it, life created is outside of God's original nature and truth—it's without His predestined and natural design. His design is true and perfect, and there are no mistakes in any of His creations because everything has purpose. Remember, *"The LORD hath made all things for himself..."* (Proverbs 16:4). Even the imperfect in man's eyes is perfect and has its purpose in the thoughts and vision of God!

As it is in the natural, so it is in the spiritual. God is the Father of all and His spiritual family of believers should be a body patterned after this same manner. Man was in relationship to God through His image, predestined for destiny through spiritual purpose on the earth. He designed that man would be birthed through his mother's womb before he entered this earthly life; however, because of sin, man can only enter into the *kingdom* (under the reign of God) if he is spiritually born again of *Water* (word/belief/baptism) and of the *Spirit* (receive the Holy Spirit). An earthly father can only create new life through God's systemic process of a natural birth—but he cannot give life of a spiritual nature (*new birth*) or make it a possibility for any of his children. That gifting is given to those who trust and believe in the promise of the Heavenly Father. He is the Father of the spiritual family, the body that grows through belief, fellowship, prayer, and spirit. He matures each believer who seeks to find the gifts that He has meticulously assigned to each. Moreover, His family of believers are not simply in the local community, but have been strategically placed throughout the world because the thoughts and visions of God are for the restoration of the entire world.

While God's initial purpose for man certainly included populating the earth, it was also important to lift up righteous men for leadership in the earth, beginning at home. Men were called to be the head (priest or covering) of his family and not simply in the physiological sense. He was called to be the spiritual leader, meaning *he* is the conduit for God's spiritual principles—instilling wisdom to the family's growth to understand the meaning of God's *true family*. He adheres to the Holy Spirit's guidance to transform and build sound foundations for a spiritual life. Most importantly, he's the thread to weave the cloak of God's love expressed toward humankind beginning with His first love in the creation of Adam.

Man's becoming the head and example before his family is an honorable position. Many accolades are often given to men when becoming a dad. The old pat on the back is conferred as the proud new father exhibits his protruding chest. A much greater admiration is bestowed on the man who stands in that distinguished position of becoming a *father*. A father takes responsibility for his children, stands accountable before them, and rears them in love and wisdom, modeling a life that is pleasing not only to him but to God. Christ often said that He and His Father are one, wanting always to demonstrate that He exhibits the will of His Father and wanting to represent Him well. A man's example should be a holy and loving life before his family, constantly reminding them of his love for God and wanting to represent Him well!

As children grow to view love, they must be treated in a pure, honest, and righteous manner so that they can distinguish between the world's view and what true love really is in the eyes of God. Life can be difficult enough without our homes adopting harmful and damaging behaviors that only display the appearance of that affection. Examples of these deceptions are: when humiliation becomes the reply for a child trusting to open up to his parents; encouragement does not start with criticism; a choice to be judgmental of a child or being pessimistic only builds a bridge of fear—creating distance. This is not the example that Christ left for displaying love! His love is light and love embraces—which neither of these examples demonstrated.

Do any of these experiences sound familiar? Remember, positive influences are always significant to growing, vibrant, and optimistic children. Allow them to view righteous judgment by handling each circumstance fairly and justly. Help them to identify that which can be controlled as well as what cannot. The Holy Scripture is God's guide to all righteousness. Even through difficult times, which consist sometimes of anger, there is a right approach and attitude for a positive outcome. Children who have yet to acquire the wisdoms surrounding the torment of anger and its damaging effects need to be taught by their fathers the mature and spiritual way to deal with such an intense emotion.

Regrettably, some children view fathers abusing that authority, using their anger as a tool for control. Fear, retribution, and condemnation are forces that poison the fiber of a character. None of the emotions of anger are positive, nor are any results of anger positive. Anger generates more anger and never demonstrates how to understand or reasonably resolve any issues without provocation. The Holy Scriptures tell us, *"And, ye fathers, provoke not your children to wrath, but bring them up in the nurture and admonition of the Lord"* (Ephesians 6:4). It is important to teach children at a young age the wisdom of God concerning parent/child relationships by directing them to Scriptures that will benefit them naturally and spiritually.

For instance, one can reference passages in the Holy Scriptures where God's love directs children to see the promises of giving parental love and proper respect: *"Children, obey your parents in the Lord: for this is right"* (Ephesians 6:1). *"Honour thy father and mother; which is the first commandment with promise; That it may be well with thee, and thou mayest live long on the earth"* (Ephesians 6:2, 3). Fathers, who display a righteous leadership and a love of God wanting to build a strong relationship with their families, exhibit the right attitude toward life by judging righteously through God's light. A loving father demonstrates how to delight and take pleasure in the life that God has given. He observes and obeys God's commandments at every point of his existence. He especially remembers to present himself as an open book, ready to reveal his vulnerabilities and to display the truth of being human—that *no one is perfect*. However, a righteous father can guide his family to know that they can experience the spiritual promises and benefits that are available through living in God's light. Then, if a family can witness and receive a benefited life through a natural father's example, how much more of a *glorious* testimony it would be if children chose to trust their father's God and Savior Jesus Christ and gain a life eternal!

Philippians 2:5 applies to all mankind, but especially men having authority in a family or in leadership of the Christian family around the world: *"Let this mind be in you, which was also in Christ Jesus." "This mind"* reflecting the mind of Christ—*let this mind* is to allow the mind to be transformed, that all men possess the same understanding—the example to follow the steps of Christ. In doing so, man takes responsibility to live by this Holy Word. Like any natural family, the church must learn to exhibit a true love by living and being a true example. We know that the church family extends far beyond a building, a nationality, a culture, or a continent, but we must embrace the same love and character, because we have a Heavenly Father whose love is offered to them all.

At times in life God will prick the heart of an individual, causing him to seek that *something more*. The reasons are not always known, but the initial steps of finding answers begins with seeking a church family that will help guide them to identify this unction in the spirit. Some who do not yet possess the indwelling of the Holy Spirit think a relationship with God is building a fellowship with man. Well, this is partly true! God does want members of the church family to have a loving relationship with one another, but can having fellowship with man promise eternal life? Only a relationship with God can fulfill that promise.

Come and allow God to prepare your heart. Dine at His table and gain strength from the sustenance of His Word. Coming to the house of God for any other reason than your belief and love for Him gains nothing. If your heart is not actively seeking God's love, joining a church body could be like enlisting in the military—becoming a part of an organization to be affixed with a noted name and activated as "Christian." At a church, you will become affixed to dead wood (a pew) and ever-gaining instructions but never equipped enough to put on the armour for the inevitable spiritual fight! To be spiritually activated, God's guidance has to be accepted and applied! Godly leaders are assigned to help new converts understand the true connection—not only assisting in duties and directions for the church, but being perceptive of the body's spiritual maturity. However, no church leader will be able to operate in these abilities without the direction of God and a character as the Bible describes in Acts 6:3, which says, "...men of honest report, full of the Holy Ghost and wisdom...." God's character can guide leadership to a position of truth, responsibility and accountability to God—not to man.

Jesus has implied these examples demonstrate our kinship of brothers and sisters. Many claim to be brothers and sisters of a church family but have neither the spirit nor the willingness to accept or embrace that whole concept of the *body*! Without the submission of our flesh and the belief in the Spirit of God, we are not His. "*So then they that are in the flesh cannot please God. ⁹But ye are not in the flesh, but in the Spirit, if so be that the Spirit of God dwell in you. Now if any man have not the Spirit of Christ, he is none of his*" (Romans 8:8, 9). As Christians, we are lacking His power to do the work of the kingdom: "*For the kingdom of God is not in word, but in power*" (1 Corinthians 4:20).

See yourself spiritually as a branch being grafted into a tree standing near living waters, bountifully offering its fruit to help nourish a kingdom work! There is work to do with the talents we've been given, but we have allowed the Enemy to sneak in and cause confusion in the spiritual family. Compromising what is right for wrong in the church family in order to enjoy our pleasures or fulfill our hidden agendas is not pleasing to the Father (e.g., lies, cover-ups, sexual sins, a form of godly appearance, etc.). These and other ungodly behaviors are debilitating and have weakened the fiber of God's body of believers. We cannot effectively draw people to the church or grow believers when we have not converted from our old ways of life.

Certainly, growing in Christ is a process, and being able to follow the ways of Christ doesn't happen overnight. Getting to the place of conversion reveals visible signs of a repentant heart! Something begins to change when a person invites God to come in. If we can obey the rules and follow the guidance of a natural father, knowing that we should expect consequences when rules are not followed, we certainly must recognize that disobeying the laws of our Heavenly Father will lead to an even heavier penalty. An unrepentant heart will cause a person's conversion to be untrue and unrepresentative of the faith. If not truly converted, a person returns to the ways of the world and sends crippling messages that damage the growth of other believers and the growth and missions of His church. That same unrepentant heart not given to God has caused even more destruction to the church's body as man's dishonesties spread to weaken not only the church, but also our countries and the world.

Man, who is called to be a good steward within the church body, takes responsibility for righteously representing the Spirit of God. *"Because it is written, Be ye holy; for I am holy"* (1 Peter 1:16). Righteousness is the characteristic that is first viewed by the world and is the integral nature that represents Christianity. For example, consider the natural family's name which points to person's heritage, his legacy, or his birthright. If a man is not conscientious in his conduct, another name will eventually attach itself to the very nature and character of that man's soul.

Have you ever heard any of these descriptions or any other such statements used to describe the character of a person in conversations? "Look out for that one! He's a piece of work," "He is not the real McCoy," "He's pretty scary or dangerous!" Whether you believe it or not, these types of statements have a way of branding themselves into the very fabric of a person's being when he is not living in righteousness. Imagine the chance of inheriting this lifelong imprint.

Again, as it is in the natural, so it is in the spiritual. This same idea applies to the family name we have already identified as followers of

Christ—Christians. (In the book of Acts, Christians were identified as "The Way" when they became followers.) Either way the name or His name should be guarded and represented well. Both Proverbs and Ecclesiastes speak to the significance of having a good name:

> "A good name is rather to be chosen than great riches, and loving favour rather than silver and gold" (Proverbs 22:1).

> "A good name is better than precious ointment; and the day of death than the day of one's birth" (Ecclesiastes 7:1).

These verses suggest that a person who possesses a good name has acquired true riches that cannot be found in material wealth. A good name is precious and invaluable. The *way* of a man's life is the lighthouse of his legacy, and these vivid memories are the ones that will shine more brightly than the day of your birth.

The world, and some Christians as well, have been influenced with the wrong idea regarding the name "Christianity." I view the use of the word "Christian" the same as the word "Roman," which identifies a person of Rome, or "Californian" in reference to an individual who resides in California. "Roman" and "Californian" simply denote where people live. Each person adopts the culture in which he lives. For example, New Yorkers have a different culture and environment than Californians because of *where they live!* As it is in the natural, so it is in the spiritual! We live in Christ and His righteousness, and the way of life for a true Christian *is* to live in holiness! Therefore, Christianity is not a religion; rather, it is a spiritual way, which demonstrates the person has adopted Christ's walk of life (cf. Deuteronomy 31:29; Isaiah 42:16, 58:2; Luke 24:35; John 14:4-6; Acts 9:2, 18:25, 19:9; Romans 11:33).

Christ brought His Father's truth to guide all mankind, particularly the life of a man and the role he fulfills as husband, father and leader; the example and witness for the man who chooses to follow Christ. Aside from knowing who he is as a person, Christianity further identifies and defines a man's spiritual path and position from the perspective of God. Christianity embodies God's light, and ability to transform the mind on the thoughts and will of God for every matter. The way of Christianity also seeks to instill spiritual qualities of God's purpose in our younger generations, teaching them that they can exercise their faith even at an earlier stage in life. This is the name "Christianity" and the mission that has been sent from the Heavenly Father.

None of this would be possible without belief in God's mission and His Son, Jesus Christ. He came to save and to bring a message of His Father's way of life as the everlasting Priest who intercedes for mankind. Jesus says that those who believe in His Father must also believe that His Father has proclaimed Him Lord and Savior. People cannot go to the Father unless they believe in Jesus and make their petitions in His name. Jesus was appointed to this position. Mankind must understand that God has given to His Son, Jesus Christ, all authority in heaven and on the earth. His name possesses confidence, manifestation, restoration, healing, edification, condemnations, proclamation, and more. His name empowers all authority, which is to be claimed by those who are not ashamed of His truth. Those believers in Christianity who truly believe in the power of His name and believe in His Father's mission for this earth make use of it!

A body of believers also uses the name "Christianity" to unite them as a family. However, Christ's way is what really unites the church body. We are God's body living out our purpose with love for one another, a mission to serve and share the blessed hope of eternal life (cf. Psalm 69:36). Through the rebirth of a believer, the family name begins to form through a belief and the image of God's spirit is found imprinted in our character. This decision allows the believer to begin journeying along the path of inheritance, now understanding that believers are children (heirs) of God and joint-heirs with Christ. They are empowered with the indwelling of the Holy Spirit and waiting in glorious hope for an eternal life with Him. God's preparation through the Holy Spirit begins to enable our gifts to do the works of His kingdom. Man can do nothing that will enhance, change, or complete this family—not through title, position, nationality, or location. Neither can anyone be elevated above any other family member.

Kingdom building is a "linking" journey, with God's serving as the first connection and ruler. Spiritually, we are simply a sister or a brother with one another through Christ Jesus. Every relationship is built through a single connection that links you and God alone—however; God may have planned a purpose for an individual journey, or have joined you with others. You may have been given a different gift or a different mission than another sister or brother, but it all comes for the work of the same mission and fitted to use where it pleases God. (cf. 1 Corinthians 12:18, 21-25). One part cannot work without the other. We all have the same opportunity to become workers for His kingdom and to receive the blessed rewards He has in store through our obedience. Please realize even your work does not position you above or beneath any other member in this family. We are from the same vine, and God is the Husbandman who grooms, trains, but also trims!

In viewing the structure and strength of family, a spiritual family can come under attack from the Adversary much like any natural family. Afflictions can come in various forms and from every direction. However, being rooted and grounded in God will help to identify the attacks, dispel its destruction, and can quickly return healing and restoration. But as truth would have it, some of the spiritual disturbances come not from outside of the church but from within. It's ignorance of God's direction; failing to invite the indwelling of the Holy Spirit, which causes the church to be under constant attack. The question should be: why are we under attack? Is the church living in God's truth, and how are God's watchmen of the church guarding the sanctity of it's walls? The Scripture says:

> "But let none of you suffer as a murderer, or as a thief, or as
> an evildoer, or as a busybody in other men's matters...[17]For
> the time is come that judgment must begin at the house
> of God: and if it first begin at us, what shall the end be of

them that obey not the gospel of God? [18]*And if the righteous*
scarcely be saved, where shall the ungodly and the sinner
appear? [19]*Wherefore let them that suffer according to the will*
of God commit the keeping of their souls to him in well doing,
as unto a faithful Creator" (1 Peter 4:15, 17-19).

The family of God must be unified, covered daily through prayer and
guided by our Heavenly Father to not adopt actions of the world. The
priest (pastor) and leadership take the charge in this effort. Godly guidance
for the church body acknowledges that a unified body in prayer is a conduit
to petition God's presence, power, blessings, and protection despite the
circumstances or appearance. For the sincere church, His protection will
not allow the world's criticisms to cause *divisions*. However, the church
leaders' responsibility is to recognize and to help heal/cleanse the parts
of the body that are functioning in unrighteousness and unholy lifestyles.
The church must understand that Christ has suffered, died, and forgiven
all of mankind's iniquities and recognize that trials and tests never has to
be dealt with alone when the church can rest in the guidance of the Holy
Spirit. Know in whom you believe, understand that God has redeemed you
to Himself. When living in righteousness and in God's light, the lessons
of failures are no longer stressors or weights but stepping-stones to God's
spiritual maturity. Otherwise, these failures continuously demonstrate
blindness within and a lack of understanding of the truth of Christ's
sacrifice. *"For if we sin willfully after that we have received the knowledge of
the truth, there remaineth no more sacrifice for sins"* (Hebrews 10:26).

All mankind have been partakers of sin before coming to accept
Christ as Lord and Savior, but not all have allowed the Holy Spirit to be
their guide toward righteous living. Man lives in sinful flesh, and every
man must strive to understand God's message of living in the light.
Otherwise, the church family will continuously have differences in its
understanding and unpredictable behaviors will persist.

For instance, a view of the church in general reveals a spiritually
divided entity. God's church has not the same message throughout the

faith. As a result, confusion and cascades of failures are within and sometimes without penalties or reproach. We should not be surprised when breakdowns take place from the mixed messages that are given throughout our churches. It is very difficult, (especially for new believers) to recognize an occurrence of actual failure when the church weakens and tolerates unrighteous behaviors.

Our Adversary rebels against God's message of truth. Nothing pleases him more than a rebellion that destroys, for then individuals totally miss the message of repentance and restoration. Unless a brother or sister has completely rejected God, he or she must stand accountable before leaders for the behaviors that do not represent God's way. Nonetheless, a person of conviction will repent, possess a humble heart, and accept whatever help he needs to be restored and made whole.

Only God can touch the heart of man, causing conviction to cut to the depths of his actions. Deep within, a spiritual consciousness is shaken causing mankind to realize the shame inflicted not only to self but also to others. Even though a person's exposure might be a harsh and shameful experience, and the work of restoration might prove to be great, we are *not* to discard him. After all, do we discard our natural family? If he is not claiming to be justifiable or is arrogant and is willing to forego the restoration process, he is not to be considered an enemy. *"If any man obey not our word by this epistle, note that man, and have no company with him, that he may be ashamed. [15] Yet, count him not as an enemy, but admonish him as a brother"* (2 Thessalonians 3:14, 15). In addition, the following instructions are directed to those whom God has given a special gift—a genuine love and compassion to convert a brother from error: *"Let him know, that he which converteth the sinner from the error of his way shall save a soul from death, and shall hide a multitude of sins"* (James 5:20). God has called all mankind to owe their love to others, but those who have been called to leadership in particular—He expects their patience, forgiveness and compassion for those hurting—wanting none to be lost.

Therefore, when man accepts the position of priesthood, whether within the church family or over his own family, a godly man assumes total reliance on God—this entails submitting to God's guidance by recognizing His truth through the leading of the Holy Spirit and His written Word. When man allows Jehovah God to rule and reign, not only is he guided to live in holiness, but he also relinquishes all attempts to move in his own ability or intellect. A prime example is when God's Word is mishandled. Being spiritually deficient, misinterpreting God's Word, and yielding only the fruit of ignorance and immaturity is a spiritual liability. Our Father has said, *"Study to shew thyself approved unto God, a workman that needeth not to be ashamed, rightly dividing the word of truth"* (2 Timothy 2:15).

Erroneous teaching of the Word further complicates the progression of spiritual movement and maturity. *"Beware lest any man spoil you through philosophy and vain deceit, after the traditions of men, after the rudiments of the world, and not after Christ"* (Colossians 2:8). Instead, allow the Holy Spirit to be a guide into all truth. Permit Him to help you identify biblical truths as opposed to emphatic views. Imparting errors cause people to judge, be confused, trigger denominational divides, generate disagreements among believers—the end result divides family members, friends, and individuals who might understand the Christian way if they could find some sense of continuity among people who proclaim truth. Jesus Christ was sent from His Father to give one message to one world: He is the same yesterday, today and forevermore. We must all understand the same: *"Now I beseech you, brethren, by the name of our Lord Jesus Christ, that ye all speak the same thing, and that there be no division among you; but that ye be perfectly joined together in the same mind and in the same judgment."* (I Corinthians 1:10)

The Holy Spirit must be invited to lead, teach, and clarify among the priesthood, or the growth of the church is hindered and more mixed messages are imparted to the world. Isaiah 48:17 says, *"Thus saith the* Lord, *thy Redeemer, the Holy One of Israel; I am the* Lord *thy God which teacheth thee to profit, which leadeth thee by the way that thou shouldest go"* (cf. Psalm 32:8, 9). The writers of such Scriptures are not advocating that man should not attend theological schools to study the Scripture and learn of God's commissions. Those who have been chosen by God have been spiritually prepared for this destiny and made ready for this journey. Christ was led by His Father to physically choose various men of diverse trades and character to be led and taught directly from Him of His Father's ways. By our standards, some of these men were quite unlikely candidates, but God's thoughts and ways are higher than ours and far surpass our understanding. He knew why He chose men of different trades, personalities, and characters for this journey. Only He can prepare such a man for purpose and destiny. Only our Heavenly Father knows the heart of man, and only the Holy Spirit can know the mind of God. He is the One who teaches what the Spirit of God wants to say or reveal. Therefore, man must recognize the connection and prepare himself to be led by the Spirit.

God's aim is to teach man to understand the benefits of a higher love and its spiritual attributes. If Adam had continued to *obey* God's commandments, his mind would have never wavered. And the peace of God would have caused righteousness to flow like a river within him. "*O that thou hadst hearkened to my commandments! then had thy peace been as a river, and thy righteousness as the waves of the sea*" (Isaiah 48:18). It's a universal and eternal truth that exists today and for evermore—that if man rest in God and surrender all in obedience, peace and righteousness are his contentment and the flow of this spirit will never end! God wants man's total surrender and dependence on Him. Then the understanding of purpose and destiny will be known. It is not for man to try to interpret or even understand the moves of God; rather, he must be willing to trust His lead. "*For my thoughts are not your thoughts, neither are your ways my ways, saith the* LORD. *⁹For as the heavens are higher than the earth, so are my ways higher than your ways, and my thoughts than your thoughts*" (Isaiah 55:8, 9).

During the beginning, there was no rationale for Adam's confusion, for only he and God communed! Nonetheless, God allowed Adam to make a choice, offering him all opportunities to possess a righteous and sustainable life. Instead Adam, even under the guidance of his Father was misled and chose to error; thus he became spiritually separated from God and blinded to His purpose. Therefore, as descendants of Adam, we all suffer in the same spiritual blindness; not knowing the path of God's destiny and the purpose of our birth. Where the garden was man's first recognition of God and his headship, sin brought about a type of *rebellion* against his Father and *Truth* that caused his separation. But rest assured that those who truly seek to find Him could be joined again as heirs! Once you find Him and really understand the meaning of the path and what it took to get there, remember it, reclaim the position, and never stray from it!

CHAPTER FIVE

LOSING SIGHT OF
RIGHTEOUS AUTHORITY

The man who possesses righteous authority also acknowledges that his position is called to submit to an even higher authority. He accepts being responsible and accountable before God. Man's spirit encompasses the image of his Heavenly Father, caring that love takes precedence for all actions demonstrated through his authority. Not only is he responsible to hear and understand God's commandments, but also spiritually accountable for preserving and obeying them. These guides established in God's commandments are the foundational pillars for acquiring the *righteous authority* needed in man.

The responsibility of a man becoming an example and priest before his family is a duty that was preordained for him before his beginning. The earth was given as man's dominion, and his care included all that God caused to exist or live, which would eventually contain his family. But man must respond to God by hearing, understanding, and acting responsibly.

In the Scriptures God promised men during their leadership and priesthood (e.g., Abraham, Isaac, etc.,) that through their acts of obedience, generations of heirs would be birthed to them. Their responsibility was to lead those generations to the patterns and ways of holiness. He is the same God today, and He is still entrusting man to become a lover and an observer of His commandments, to sear them into his memory, and to brand their words on the table of his heart. Being responsible for following the commands is assuming that righteous authority—thereby fulfilling God's promises toward building a spiritually sound foundation for family. Our God's decrees offer guidance to holiness that will present righteous living for family and relationships. When God's commandments are practiced in actual living, man's understanding of these instructions began to activate his movements in spirituality—eventually reflecting a life, which benefits from these valued life choices (many of which are found in Proverbs). Our Father will open the understanding to true riches, treasures, and the wisdom of life—just a few of the advantages promised to those who live in His light. These foundations represent man's responsibility to begin his spiritual *building* for God. They are solid pillars for building and developing righteous and healthy lives—setting godly examples before generations of families.

Man's righteous authority also encompasses accountability—first to *God*, to *himself* and then his *family*. With accountability comes strength to exercise his becoming liable, being exposed, being answerable, and being truthful—even if it causes him to stand alone. At times, standing for righteousness may seem to be a solitary and lonely act, but when standing for God in accountability, a person is never left alone. This position declares, "Yes! I will submit to His guidance and to a calling for righteous authority to have purpose and life." Jesus Christ came to the earth with purpose—to give the message of His Father's truth. He knows man faces an earthly battle and only the *strength in truth* will oppose our Adversary. Many times Christ stood on the words of His Father's truth, trusted and fought the Enemy despite the overwhelming circumstances.

The Adversary would like nothing more than to cause man to crumble under pressure and opt out of a work or situation that should be owned. A great leader demonstrates that strength is not simply in knowing truth but also in living and becoming a product of truth. Some of the most indelible teachings in life come through trials where accountability was owned. Through these experiences, God allows truth and wisdom to help mold character. Practices of becoming accountable to God's commandments can test the believer's faith, and how he goes through the test or trial will determine his level of maturity.

Teaching a family that life, which surrounds us, is in constant change is so important. Nothing is certain; not even man is a surety. Lives can be set up for failure when total trust is placed in man; he is not perfect, and the circumstances of the future or its outcome are not in his control. Choose rather to be confident and accountable to God, and through His will, the circumstances will work out exactly as they should! We don't necessarily see or feel God's movement, but trusting and *expecting* God's affects offers great promise. Making right choices and being accountable for living by holy principles allow us to see His promises manifest. Responsibility and accountability are not tangible; rather, they are a conviction of the soul and a mental transformation—an intangible reminder of God's great gift to choose what He has already placed within. They are infused within man's image to follow that perfect example (Christ Jesus) and being answerable to a holy and higher calling.

Can our Father really trust man to choose well? He has given man stewardship and authority over the realm of the earth, but can it be said that he has been accountable for being a good steward of his spiritual and natural body, the earth, the atmosphere, one another, his government, or the people of all nations? When man can find himself to be responsible and accountable to manage all things in a purpose of love, he begins to spiritually understand, that circumstances in life are less about himself and all about God. As we can see, most men have not been called to be a priest of the church. However, every man has been called and given an opportunity to live Christ's way and become a good steward and example to live a holy priesthood.

The word *integrity* comes to mind regarding a man who cares to be accountable to self. When no one is around to view your actions, do you conscientiously uphold a moral standard and spiritual principle because it is right? Recognize that there is no hiding from or deceiving our Creator. Man is accountable to a God who sees not as he does, because God views the heart (cf. 1 Samuel 16:7). Whatever the circumstance, unlike your fellow man, God knows your true thoughts. A man who is accountable carefully examines his every decision, knowing that every choice that's placed into action begins to spiritually carve a pathway for his future. Whether positive or negative, the reward or consequences of those choices await their appointed time for return—usually when least expected!

God is for man's choosing the higher and spiritual principle of action when facing any obstacles. With the Holy Spirit for guidance, he will understand who and what lies behind every circumstance—God will cause every issue to clearly come into view. At times it may seem that obstacles are approaching on every side, and at these moments, man must rest confident in God's Word. *"And he said unto me, My grace is sufficient for thee: for my strength is made perfect in weakness…"* (2 Corinthians 12:9).

Living and depending on God's principles is truly beneficial, an assurance that His empowerment will always get you through your weakest moments—not only at your weakest but for every effort or challenge. Because the Father loves his children, decide to make every action (and thought) pleasing by carefully honoring and making righteous decisions.

+ Have control of impure thoughts or desires, keeping them from coming to realization.
+ Understand that no guilt can exist long enough, before it's destroyed with the confession of truth.
+ No outside attractions or other desires are strong enough to lure you away from God's precious treasures already in your possession.
+ You know that anything that goes against God's truth, are the adversary's deceptions.

Don't be deceived or allow yourself to be led onto the crooked and wide path. What waits is the inevitable penalty of destruction!

Finally, any man who accepts accountability to himself is also accountable to his family. Only through an intimate relationship with God can a man know the plans and purposes that the Father has for his family. The family as a unit, or each individual, can be guided through life if the head is in the right position. Man's relationship must be one that is open, honest, and pure with God in every facet of life, before he can establish such exposure before his family. Man must recognize the fact that errors are inevitable because he is imperfect. Many times the Scriptures share examples of leadership's displaying vulnerabilities, but a godly leader will own it. No matter the liability, the weakness, or the exposure, whether that path was a diversion or purposed, he recognizes the situation as another opportunity to learn and mature. This approach can also be seen as a tool—not simply a lesson for yourself, but also a testimony that will be impactful for others to grow.

As a godly leader before a family, man's responsibility is to identify and guard his family against ungodly behaviors, even if those behaviors are found within him. God has created and formed each man the same, but because of various personalities, each man can possess a character that is *unique*. Uniqueness is a form of the character that expresses individuality. Because the flesh is imperfect, individuality can give way to an *eccentric charm* in some people that occasionally is considered unconventional. That personality certainly stands out among others, but is not necessarily harmful. Yet, there are others with character flaws displaying harmful and offensive behavior. These characteristics should never be ignored as simply unique. We were created to edify one another by loving and supporting one another through weakness—not through damaging another's spirit or inflicting pain. The uniqueness in man does not determine what is right or wrong. Man does!

When a man professes that he lives in Christ and errors, his spirit is touched in a place of immediate remorse, leading him to repentance.

This type of response is righteous, and reveals a good, sound example that molds a strong spiritual family unit. A father is not merely a man who is to be visible in the home; he is also an example to emulate, one who imprints a divine map of God's love on the heart of every member of his family. His example is a legacy being imparted to family and a generation he may never witness!

Generally, a person's initial introduction to authority is experienced through the family. Therefore, laying a sound foundation to establish children's trust for authority in their early years is significant. This groundwork molds and establishes respect for authority later in life. When a man is demonstrating leadership God's way, he will not misuse his authority with discouraging behavior, provoking anger and displaying fits of rage. Instead, his method will demonstrate how to first revere and depend on God in all matters. He will help to provide good decision-making skills as the encourager who is always supportive in times of need. He also recognize God has established earthly authority—by demonstrating the importance of respecting the given powers and authorities that have also been ordained of God for the earth (cf. Romans 13:1, 2, 6, 7).

A father's position acknowledges that leadership and authority is not merely limited to his family but by applying God's truths in living with others. These foundations are essential to viewing life with a spiritual eye. His actions are guided from above as he carefully exhibits healthy behaviors and spiritual goodness as an example of life through God's eyes. Without these spiritual possessions governing his actions, it is impossible to view the commands of God. However, being ignorant of His principles can result in unrighteous conduct going undetected. Hence, unmanaged behaviors can only result in this logical conclusion: when a person is repeatedly exposed to an unhealthy environment, he can only produce damaged and broken individuals who are doomed to cause a ripple of consequences for succeeding generations.

Example of Ungodly Behavior

> "...*They that be whole need not a physician, but they that*
> *are sick*" (Matthew 9:12).

When a person has been wronged, ignoring his hurt and moving on is dishonorable. To make such a choice destroys trust and begins a spiritual disconnect. This pattern is the antithesis of the love that God wants man to share.

I have already alluded to man's behaviors being owned. Many dynamics and elements of mankind's nature are not a deciding factor, but not owning behavior should not be one of them. Man's behavior is to his choosing and not owning something that is problematic, gives the Adversary an open invitation to cause destruction. He is a destroyer of character, the author of confusion and a delighter in collapsing the integrity of any relationship. Not owning an error leads to hiding and finding fault or blaming others.

Do your part by immediately asking for forgiveness from those whom you have offended or hurt. Seek God's forgiveness (because we are all His children) and leave the judging to Him. After all, you are following His order for good relationships!

> "*Therefore if thou bring thy gift to the altar, and there*
> *rememberest that thy brother hath ought against thee;*
> *[24]Leave there thy gift before the altar, and go thy way; first*
> *be reconciled to thy brother and then come and offer thy*
> *gift.*" (Matthew 5:23, 24; cf. Matthew 5:25, 26; Proverbs
> 18:19 and Psalm 86:5).

In viewing another perspective, persons making the choice to ignore and simply move on fail to address the problem. Too many times pride drives man's decision to ignore wrongdoing. Prolonging unsolved issues only fuels anger. If a matter is not settled immediately, he could end up paying for his actions for years to come (cf. Luke 12:58). Freeing oneself of the guilt and shame takes owning truth and humbling yourself before God and man. The responsibility is simply to choose what is right and replace actions of disgrace with good things! With all of the negativity in this world, man (or mankind) must own his part to restore and fill it with good. What does taking this avenue of replenishing the earth really mean? Well, from the beginning God's plan involved Adam and Eve being fruitful, multiplying, and filling the earth with good people of His perfected light. God had intended that all would live and revere Him as a loving Heavenly Father, with an additional purpose of serving one another.

The American Heritage Dictionary defines replenish as "to fill or make complete again." Spiritually, this definition applies to all things that God created, especially people. Replenishing has "the purpose of making something or someone filled (or fulfilled) or made whole or complete." God knows that the human experience requires relationships. Any relationship that has been stressed must be restored to spiritual wholeness; where spirit and body are full and raised to a level of functionality. Our total being should reflect the true essence of God's light that will allow us to experience wholeness.

Few understand that all mankind must possess this same light, remaining at a spiritual level designed for habitation. However, committing sins against God and toward others dims that light. Only a repentant heart and forgiveness can restore a person to shine as brightly as the sun! A true confession is a heart cleanser and a purifier that begins its filtering through honesty. Our Heavenly Father desires all of us to be restored to that level of light. Without love and forgiveness, it's an impossibility. Remember, He loved and forgave mankind, and mankind must do the same for one another.

Let your light shine. Stand boldly and be accountable. And wherever someone's light has been diminished, help that person to replenish the light with love. Be restored to wholeness so that the tools, which God has gifted within you, can be used for His glory.

What is His light? Allow me to illustrate by means of a puzzle. Without every single piece of the puzzle, its missing pieces will reflect holes, and the puzzle will never reveal the complete picture or the story that is meant to capture your imagination. In other words, a puzzle is never complete without all of its pieces. In God's view of humanity, the holes from the missing pieces represent places where one of His righteous characteristics is missing—love, selflessness, honesty, neighborliness, kindness, truth and friendship.

Man has been marvelously and wonderfully made in God's image, but at times, God's image is definitely not reflected in man's character. Without that reflection, man cannot accomplish the plans for which He has been equipped. Sin hinders the service to God. Possessing a righteous character recognizes that any wrongdoing against another person must be made right to begin a healing—not simply to rid oneself of the guilt—but for others to be restored to the original level of God's wholeness. Again, man was created to be a picture of love and light in this universe, yet with so many gaping holes, the view of His "light" is nonexistent when seen by others *"Let your light so shine before men, that they may see your good works, and glorify your Father which is in heaven"* (Matthew 5:16).

The world is most certainly watching and taking note when Christians display ungodly behaviors! Even more, these uncorrected behaviors (particularly among persons of authority) can influence or impact multitudes to follow that same example. Man must recognize that God's mercies are extended to all mankind, and all live daily by His grace. Man must truly live in righteousness so that others may see the *love* (light) of God reflected in his character (cf. Romans 13:8-10; John 13:35). Therefore, it's man's responsibility is to be cognizant of behavior, especially in the presence of our youth or the young in Christ. He must choose to be led by Christ's example where all mankind is given a righteous conduct for living. Living His way will divert man from the errors that torment and diminish souls. Paul's prayer was that all *"May be able to comprehend with all saints what is the breadth, and length, and depth, and height; [19]And to know the love of Christ, which passeth knowledge, that ye might be filled with all the fullness of God"* (Ephesians 3:18, 19).

We must all stay connected by caring for one another because the day will come when *"...every one of us shall give account of himself to God"* (Romans 14:12). Therefore, correcting behaviors that have gone amiss replenishes the Spirit and builds the faith and trust needed in one another. This is the *image* of God's original dream for mankind's *love*.

CHAPTER SIX

MAN VIEWS A MARRIAGE; GOD VIEWS A HOLY UNION

"*Whoso findeth a wife findeth a good thing, and obtaineth favour of the LORD*" (Proverbs 18:22). The Scripture reveals that God did not think it would be good for man to be alone in the world. All of His living creatures had mates except for man; hence, His imagination of Eve became an actuality and Adam's mate (help meet)—a blessed, purposeful, and complete complement for God's human union.

The verse implies that *man* (by the leading of the Lord) is the one to find his wife and not visa versa. Therefore, if God presented the women to Adam, then follow the pattern and allow Him to present your wife. However, while in waiting, a woman's calling is to allow God to prepare and preserve her until that appointed time—because God is guiding the man to "*findeth a wife.*" If God's ordained order is adhered to and followed, God has but one-way to respond—favorably! It's painful to witness failures of mankind's effort, where God was left out of this process and marriages were *formed* but were not *spiritually joined.* It was man that was given woman to be joined in marriage, but he must seek God first to find that righteous woman for this holy union. A man's relationship with God helps him to be spiritually guided, preparing his heart to recognize when she is revealed to him. God's knows the Christ-like character in a woman, like Christ knows the heart of the church for His bride. It is through man's desire to please his Father that his discernment is allowed to recognize the spirit filled (Holy Spirit) character in a woman—a converted life made ready to work in harmony. In her, he finds not only his love but a friend, a complement, a companion, a nurturer, a supporter, an encourager, and a bearer of life—not simply life in bearing children—but a spring welling up with joy, delight, and goodwill, always a sharer of love in her encounters. The Scripture refers to these treasures that God plants within her as a *"good thing."*

Typically, a woman who is preparing for marriage and loves God is drawn to love a man who serves God. In her view, a husband who serves God is committed to holy living in marriage, and as Scripture has said in I Peter 1:15, in *"all manner of conversation"* or interpreted as "with every part of his existence." Therefore, aside from the love that bonds man's adoration to God, man's initial commitment to bond as one begins with his wife. This devotion is an act of love that should be cherished, praying continuously to bless her actions in all that her hands do, especially for the work of the kingdom. Bestowing this kind of love, which develops trust and builds a pillar of strength that is relied upon through difficulty, will guide their union with wisdom throughout life. This agape love binds a husband and a wife in power that no man can put asunder.

However, to experience that kind of love in marriage, man must demonstrate his love for God through faith. He must have the faith to believe with confidence that the Holy Scripture is the Word of God. All of what God has said in Scripture regarding creation is true, including the creation of marriage. From the beginning He brought together His two human creations to bond in marriage, and the two became one body (natural and spiritual) fitted together. His opposites were created and called to work together for a purpose. Without this process, the truth is ignored, preventing His natural order for life and the new births that are meant to come through that bonding of a husband and wife (cf. Genesis 1:28). This scriptural union was created and blessed by our God—to be *"fruitful, and multiply and replenish."*—a commandment with purpose and destiny for populating the earth with people of innate wholeness.

Although the biological design of creation still holds true, some families are not birth out of a marriage, but are created with love and acceptance. In God's image, we are created to care for one another as family. Scripture has shown us that from love, families also were created through other means—such as David's counting Nathan closer than any brother and at the crucifixion when Jesus gave John the care of His mother.

Families can be formed through many life situations, such as adoption, inheritance, and guardianship. Yet, if we believe, we must understand that all things created by Him are true and are indeed perfect and purposeful, including His predestined plan (or pattern) for creating families. Nonetheless, our Father loves us, and He desires all of us to experience a family environment that exhibits support, care, and divine love, which is vital for our connection. This connection is difficult, however—because of sin man is blinded from seeing our Father's spiritual truths, and he cannot discern Satan's deceits regarding the creation of family. Satan also invites us to view negative and damaging replicas as alternatives for families.

Anything that does not demonstrate truth and love and is birthed out of hatred is not a family—gangs, cults, cliques, dogmatic religions, etc. Satan *never* changes; he has used these same tactics since Creation. He used them against Adam and Eve when he attacked them as family. He takes part of the truth and twists it to undermine God so that the thinking is eventually clouded, blocking God's light and truth. If entertained long enough, Satan's tactics and deceptions will always appear believable, and if believed, they will eventually become man's truth!

> *And the* Lord *God commanded the man, saying, "Of every tree of the garden thou mayest freely eat:* [17]*But of the tree of the knowledge of good and evil, thou shalt not eat of it: for in the day that thou eatest thereof thou shalt surely die.* [3:1]*Now the serpent was more subtle than any beast of the field which the* Lord *God had made. And he said unto the woman, Yea, hath God said, Ye shall not eat of every tree of*

the garden? ⁴*And the serpent said unto the woman, Ye shall not surely die."* (Genesis 2:16, 17; 3:1, 4)

To say that we have the kind of faith that pleases God says that we trust the truth of His Word for *all things.* The truth is that God loves us all, but He hates *all* sin, including what we believe are the "minor" sins (including, but not limited to, lies, gossips, cheating, etc.); these and all sin are indeed deplorable to God. When living in God's light, no secrets are hidden from the sincere heart seeking truth. God will reveal it *all* to those who genuinely seek Him for answers; they are there for the asking! The choice belongs to man; he must come with a sincere heart asking and believing. Through belief the Holy Spirit is released to confirm God's truth of all things in life—even the sins of the man seeking. We must read Scripture and allow God's Word to permeate our spirit with truth and conviction. Through God, the Holy Spirit is ultimately the Teacher, Comforter, and Judge—not man (cf. John 16:7-11).

> *"For I know nothing by myself; yet am I not hereby justified: but he that judgeth me is the Lord. Therefore judge nothing before the time, until the Lord come, who both will bring to light, the hidden things of darkness, and will make manifest the counsels of the hearts: and then shall every man have praise of God"* (1 Corinthians 4:4, 5).

More importantly, the entire human mission is not simply about bonding in marriage but building loving relationships because of our need for one another. But possessing a loving relationship where it speaks to marriage is especially important—where God's intended opposites are essential for building one harmonious (complete) union. Where is the effort and challenge to labor and build continuity in something with which you are already familiar? This design and destiny was chosen to be the journey for the husband and wife's oneness—a blending of his physical strength, her delicateness; his constructiveness, her analysis; his resolve, her tolerance; his sperm, her womb; etc.—all working together to create God's perfect purpose, plan, and destiny in the world.

Although we recognize that man and woman were created as opposites and made to serve in different capacities, we are equally important to God's common purpose. Since the beginning, man and woman were made to fulfill the union by each complementing the other in ways they were not equipped. The ultimate plan of the Father was for the two to blend and become one and complete. God wants every couple to understand that His calling the wife to "submit" is not an inferiority posturing but a purposeful position of God's choosing (cf. Ephesians 5:23 God's positioning of husband and wife) that she will follow her husband as he follows Christ. Again, he is the head of his wife as Christ is the head of the church. She is content in his decisions, knowing that God has ordered every step he makes.

Both husband and wife having respect for the other's position, align themselves with God's command, "Love ye one another." When possessing an agape love for others, we trust God for the spiritual move of the relationship. Such was the confidence that Sarah had in her husband, Abraham. *"Even as Sara obeyed Abraham, calling him lord..."* (1 Peter 3:6). This passage of Scripture demonstrates that Sarah trusted God and clearly had respect for her husband Abraham's position. She always acknowledged his headship and trusted God for his every move as he fulfilled the priesthood over his family. Yet, like in many marriages where God grows us, at times life challenges try our faith. It is true that Sarah failed miserably at one point in trusting her husband, to wait on God's timing for the promised child. She was old, doubtful, and impatient and resorted to natural thinking. We fail to remember that God's thoughts are higher than our thoughts. She was like many of us today! We say that we trust God, but when we are going through our trial, we try to help Him out. Clearly, God does not need our help. Impatience averts His timing (which is always perfect), and we can bring anguish upon ourselves as Sarah did when she finally had a child as promised—but at what cost? Her impatience to "help" God, presenting her maiden Hagar to Abraham, later brought on jealousy, anguish, and confusion. She doubted the word of Abraham—overlooking that Abraham received his instruction from God. Even though Sarah's faith exposed struggles of weakness, she did trust her husband and knew that Abraham walked with God!

Why should men invite the fellowship of God to rule and reign over his marriage? He not only directs you toward building a solid bond, but He also demonstrates how to have a righteous fellowship and authority over your marriage. Because of sin, man has already gained a fallen character—if he is not spiritually grounded, he can quite easily take this as a position of advantage or superiority, allowing pride and narcissism to seep in through leadership and authority. But a headship that invites the guidance of God recognizes that all strength and power is wrapped in harmony to operate in *love*.

Many of today's marriages struggle to be morally and spiritually sound. Some are built on marital agreements that express no love, simply spoken or written innuendos that already suggest a marital defeat even before the marriage begins. A marriage should be brought together honestly and spiritually with a bond that radiates a passion of love and righteousness—a bond that God respects. If the relationship is not honest and true, the facade will be as transparent as glass!

Becoming the *one flesh* that Scripture speaks about in a marriage is not impossible. However, this oneness includes God and comes from a genuine and sincere love affair. Such a love ties together the mind, body, and soul. It's a oneness where husbands recognize their wives as themselves. *"So ought men to love their wives as their own bodies. He that loveth his wife loveth himself"* (Ephesians 5:28). This oneness joins all that a husband and a wife are to one another to feel each other's joy, pain, dreams or anticipations—all because the connection that honors God, strengthens the love that binds. God wants this spiritual tie or *oneness* between a husband and wife, and *"…let not man put [it] asunder"* (Matthew 19:6).

A husband's relationship with his wife is meant to be sacred and pure, and one so connected that *no one can pull it apart*. However, a husband allowing impure thoughts, views, desires, or imprudent contact from outside influences can lead to marital endangerment. God knows every man individually because He created him. When the Disciples of Christ asked Him how they should pray, He gave them the perfect prayer, knowing what was needed for their physical and spiritual wholeness. The prayer included the phrase, *"And lead us not into temptation..."* (Matthew 6:13). This element of the prayer points to the many weaknesses and temptations of mankind's flesh (in particular when living for Christ), especially that of sexual impurity, which has been insidiously used to damage relationships since creation.

The body has been masterfully designed to respond the same in everyone—all bleed when cut, all share the same human suffering during sickness, and all experience the same sexual desires. The sexual sensors of the body can be naturally set in motion during any instance of sentuality, whether consciously or unconsciously; it was created as a *normal* body response. However, God's divine order is that the actual practice of intimacy be sanctioned, reserved and shared only within the blessed union of the marriage. If a man's sexual desires are not under control, they can lure him into unhealthy and sometimes dangerous sexual circumstances. Intimacy or sexuality is psychosomatic; it seizes the mind, which is why man requires no effort to recall an intimate experience—a bonding that creates a type of soul tie. What's hidden is this: the danger in tying your soul and sexual experiences with every individual with whom they have been intimately involved. What does that mean? Intimacy hitches the emotions of the souls together through a link of every sexual familiarity—a sacred link that should be reserved and accessed only through marriage. The Scripture says, *"...to avoid fornication, let every man have his own wife, and let every woman have her own husband"* (1 Corinthians 7:2). Linking such familiarities is connecting body, soul, and spirit—even smells, looks, sounds, touch—or any other familiar emotions, are triggers that can recollect experiences of immoral soul ties.

Despite how sex is regarded by mankind and today's social standards, engaging in intimacy outside of the marriage is an act of adultery. Intimacy within the confines of adultery is an entanglement of mixed emotions and bliss, creating fantasy passions that are disingenuous and impure. Remember, the body reacts naturally and normally in sexual situations, therefore, the body is not at fault. You alone must determine if the body is reacting in the appropriate setting! Again, the Scripture demonstrates that attractions are natural and created with a purpose. However, these affections should be placed under control or *contained* if the individuals are not married. *"But if they cannot contain, let them marry: for it is better to marry than to burn"* (1 Corinthians 7:9). This verse states that it is better to marry and freely express your sexual desires with your own spouse than to burn with lustful desires, which can lead to fornication—or when married, adultery. Fornication occurs when two people not married to each other join together in sexual intimacy. The Scripture clarifies, *"What? know ye not that he which is joined to an harlot is one body? for two, saith he, shall be one flesh"* (I Corinthians 6:16). Often fornication becomes a repetitive behavior, leading to patterns of sexual addiction.

Of great importance is giving attention to how you enter your relationships and how you make your connections. New relationships, especially those between a man and a woman, should simply be of a friendly nature, showing kindness and respect, conducting yourself as a good neighbor. Allow time to grow your friendship through social interactions while you become knowledgeable and grow trust for individuals. Always express respectfulness and decency in your relationship.

A man whose marriage expresses agape love understands the value of his blessings and will not entertain desires that would interrupt his blessed union. The gratefulness is living for Christ, which, through transformation, acknowledges that his body must be set apart as His temple. A man who honors this, keeps the body under submission by meditating on the content of His Word. Never chance your good character and position to be compromised by carelessly exposing yourself in precarious and ungodly territory; they are traps placed by the Enemy to always lead to a person's detriment. Making a righteous decision is up to man (cf. 1 Corinthians 10:13).

In serving a holy God, light and dark cannot share the same space. In 2 Corinthians 6:14, the Scripture says, *"Be ye not unequally yoked together with unbelievers: for what fellowship hath righteousness with unrighteousness? and what communion hath light with darkness?"* Sharing a life with someone who doesn't see Christ as the Truth expresses a different view in his/her belief and has no respect for divine principles. And the spouse living with a non-believer can practically rule out their accountability—trust can be a major shortcoming when attempting to build a bond. Instances where adultery comes into play will be hidden or accepted as part of life's shifts that merely—happen!

Adultery is an abandonment of your marriage, thinking selfishly of a temporary gratification without even a thought of the outcome. Consumed thoughts and desires finally become a reality when they are no longer thoughts, but acts! Living for Christ means that He entirely governs your life, even your sensuality. Affections and caring are emotions created in our character for the enjoyment of any relationship, but intimacy and sensuality is sacred and pure, reserved only for your holy union. Unrighteousness cannot share in holy living, but no sin is so great that God cannot forgive—if those involved in adultery are truly repentant and are rejoined through reconciliation.

A person considering marriage should be led to remain pure by the indwelling of the Holy Spirit. Abstaining from sexual relationships before marriage not only pleases God, but abstinence will also please you, knowing that your marriage began pure. Entering a pure intimacy is the glorious part of bonding (like our worship to God) that should only be shared with that special one! A righteous, holy and inherently spiritual ties to the other. No other earthly person can share the depths of this transcendent place that you both consecrate as holy. Others outside, entering this marital bond, will cause pure and honest emotions to become more complicated and torturous (comparing, preferences, yearns, etc.)—emotions become questionable and or disloyal.

Husband, understand that loving your wife as yourself is significant to growing and maturing your bond. Understand that love grows spousal respect and, more importantly, intimacy in the marriage. Intimacy is most often misinterpreted as a focus solely on sex, while the more important expression is ignored altogether. The spiritual closeness is what really creates intimacy or an intimate environment. God teaches that love builds a spiritual closeness within marriage—illustrating that the same love and spiritual closeness He desires to exist with mankind. An example is when we pray to God and spend time with Him. We create this type of intimacy or closeness because we share our love and hearts through our fellowship. Through a true worship and praise, raises a type of glory, exaltation, splendor, and beauty of His holiness. A sweet savor (spiritual incense) is raised and can only be understood by God through a pure heart's devotion. This love expression is the same toward a wife. The Scripture says, "*So ought men to love their wives as their own bodies. He that loveth his wife loveth himself. ²⁹For no man ever yet hated his own flesh; but nourisheth and cherisheth it, even as the Lord the church*" (Ephesians 5:28, 29).

Since one of man's purposes was to be in authority, daily he should reflect and examine himself, asking, "How do I treat my relationships?" (Matthew 22:39, "*…love thy neighbour as thyself.*") However, he should be especially cognizant of this authority and love in his marital relationship by asking, "God, give me wisdom as to how to love my wife and to build a relationship that pleases You." A husband's every thought and action should be done with the consideration of his spouse. Aside from the love of God, no greater affection should be shared than that which a husband has established with his wife.

Detachment and prioritizing are more areas to review when creating oneness in a marriage. One of the first acts that God demanded of man in preparation for his marriage was that he must *leave* (detach from) his father and mother. The Scripture states, "*Therefore shall a man leave his father and his mother, and shall cleave unto his wife…*" (Genesis 2:24). He is prepared to leave the guidance and nurturing of his beginnings to become one with the woman God has guided him to choose as his mate. He has grown through the knowledge acquired from the parents of his youth; now he must trust his spiritual Father to help guide his new relationship toward their eternal life.

It is also important to *prioritize* your new life—your marriage relationship versus outside relationships. Prioritizing doesn't mean that you abandon the affections of your previous life (unless they truly need abandoning), but it does imply re-adjusting. Creating the kind of intimacy that God wants for a marriage takes time—especially with spending more time with the Father for guidance and reserving time to acquaint and understand one another. As important as the marriage is, attention to *how* you build this new relationship takes time and care; it is the pinnacle to your union. Allow God to be the foundation of your marriage and give Him His time and reverence for molding a holy union.

Through time comes a direction for your walk together. A husband must give ample time to prayer, communication, leisure, and serving. He is to be responsible and accountable to his wife and a positive influence and example to others. Fulfilling these tasks takes time. Where his life was once single, he is now married and no longer in the single arena. Where his plans once entailed only one, his present life plans includes two. Whereas he once had single friends, he is now acquainted with more couples. Building this kind of union with the guidance of God can create an experience of true intimacy that reaches far beyond the *physical*. These connecting developments only exist when the marriage is a top priority and becomes the focal point to building a holy union.

Equally as important as the physical and spiritual is creating intimacy in your environment. Open and unspoken invitations speak to closeness and harmony with another person. A simple closeness or a display of open and spontaneous affection creates a loving and intimate environment. This act could be as simple as washing a dish, staying in the same room with the loved one, placing a kiss on the cheek, making a loving phone call, offering support, communicating, sending flowers, or simply walking hand in hand. Get the point? *Intimacy* is simply "an

honest display of a devoted spirit constantly illustrating an alluring love
for one another—demonstrating Christ's love, a couple's affections can
be sincere and authentic."

Giving thought to creating an intimate environment is a constant
effort that is a must to establishing oneness. Even amid conversations
with others, it's important to create this atmosphere by remembering to
be respectful and cognizant of your relationship. Allow your speech for
one another to be proper and kind. Your words are powerful energy and
are cyclical. A positive statement will in turn generate a positive response;
likewise, a negative statement will generally elicit a negative reply. Making
respectful remarks concerning your spouse generates a respectful and
receptive environment—creating that positive environment can influence
openness with the freedom to inspire. They are virtues that will earn
admiration from others. This type of intimate environment grows love
and trust, and is so liberating that it will surely elevate your marriage to
a level that others will admire and duly respect.

However, this intimacy cannot exist in environments that consist
of selfishness, insensitivity, cruelty, and fear. This behavior does not
create a liberating environment and can only generate bitterness and
hatred, which if not corrected, will invariably create many offenses. The
Scripture says, *"There is no fear in love; but perfect love casteth out fear:
because fear hath torment. He that feareth is not made perfect in love"* (1
John 4:18). The character of love was illustrated perfectly for us through
Christ. His purpose demonstrated genuine love through the examples
of caring for one another, and showing the benefits of building spiritual,
loving, and lasting relationships. Fear and all of its negative onslaughts
inflicts poison, sickens the physical body and hinders our spiritual
growth so that it prevents the advancement in each of our purposes. Fear
restricts the body and inflicts stressors that will not only begin to create
diseases, but will also hinder spiritual efforts by creating screens that
hide the visions of God's divine plan. Man is not free in his spirit when
he possesses a disturbed mind. His anxieties can delay or terminate

a destiny, and all of the manifestations that could have been released through the blessed gifts he holds.

The only healthy fear is the fear of God (a reverence), and the only healthy hatred is the hatred of evil. He says, *"The fear of the LORD is to hate evil: pride, and arrogancy, and the evil way, and the froward mouth, do I hate"* (Proverbs 8:13). In some parts of our world, the males of some countries and cultures still practice the meaningless and harsh practice of brutally controlling women as a way of demonstrating to society that they manage their household or exhibit their authority in headship. In actuality, managing should always begin with self.

Arrogance, cruelty, the lack of sympathy, insensitivity, un-forgiveness, abrasiveness, and blaring speech all become a part of the arsenal used to gain control and possession. No man owns another in God's eyes, but this fact cannot be truer than it is for the relationship that was sanctioned by God called marriage. God has created woman for man, and as seen in Scripture, He has called man to recognize the woman as himself and as a companion by being joined to her in harmony and love. This blending of the soul, mind, and belief enables the *pair* to move in the same direction. Scripture calls it becoming "equally yoked" (cf. 2 Corinthians 6:14). In biblical times when a yoke of oxen was paired together for work in the field, they were generally the same dimensions. One did not tower over the other, or the walk would become erratic or jerky, causing their ability to work together to become more complicated or even impossible. The Christian walk is not easy in this world, and a Christian couple's walk can be even more difficult if the two do not see themselves as one. Either way, their walk should demonstrate an example of lessons and love taught by a divine *Teacher*—that they are no longer two but *one flesh.*

Even though man was born into a world of sin, Christ has been the example and offers another way. But the times when man ignores His offer, he repeats the same errors and suffers the same penalties. The Scripture continually illustrates that there is no new thing under the sun. Sin still exists, and unless man follows God, he will continue to experience sinful ways to error. Man's causing others to suffer for his own frailties or behaviors is as old as the beginning (e.g., Eve blamed Satan, and Adam in turn, blamed Eve for their fallen state).

Man was created to be the priest of his life and home, to stand strong and accountable when necessary, and not place blame on the one given to stand by him. The man who places burdens on the wife for his weakness is exactly that—weak. His burdens are being inflicted at her expense. Love is not a life of condemnation, which generates fear, low self-esteem, indecisiveness, and a lack of confidence. Where is the show of love and the equal walk that has been commanded of Christ in such a behavior?

In time, our precious Father in heaven had compassion to forgive woman for her sin, but it seems that some men still wrestle with this act of godliness. Therefore, his spirit continues to conflict his soul. For centuries, some customs have placed much strife on women, e.g., being required to completely hide their body in public, serving as the sexual dumping ground for men's superstitious beliefs, enduring genital mutilations, suffering foot bindings, and/or various other bodily disfigurements. In many cultures women are in the majority, but they still have fewer rights, including no right to an education, or to vote, or even to travel without the male's approval. These and other acts have been performed for centuries, and none of them has ever had any rational benefits. They are perpetrated merely for the sake of status, pride, and tradition, though some implications have coupled them with religious purposes. In actuality, embracing such practices is a depiction of control. Generally, when a controller inflicts fear and frailties onto one, it's certain to expose the weaknesses of that perpetrator—usually some form of insecurity. These inflictions however, are the powerful forces which label women as *less than*. It is a grave assumption to think, "If you lessen the women's attraction, you lessen a man's reaction." Stressors and insecurities bring out all sorts of issues, which are the driving forces of fear. In actuality, fear of losing control and his inherent weaknesses motivate his anxieties.

Again, love does not hurt. Causing others to live in strife and bondage does not free or elevate another. In fact, more stressors and grief are placed on the jailer than on the one who is jailed. The jailer has now acquired not only the many efforts of managing the one he has imprisoned but also the added stress and labor of controlling the rebellious spirits of those on whom he has inflicted pain. An environment created that breeds confrontation and friction within this harsh prison confine (much like the work required in ruling the Israelite slaves in Exodus 1:11-14).

Today man must remember and shift his thinking from the transgressions and frailties from the days of his ancient past. He must live, learn, and mature to know that Christ has liberated *all of us*. The New Testament teaches that mankind has been restored, and God has reconciled *all* back to Himself through our faith in Jesus Christ. We all have liberty if we live righteously in Him (cf. Galatians 3:19, 24-29; 2 Corinthians 5:17). Man and woman once had the sanctity of a sacred haven—an intimate environment created for their living. His infinite love existed there for all of His creation, and His children experienced light and truth in a paradise of provision and perfection. God wants a husband to create, provide and enjoy this same liberty in a loving paradise when joined in marriage.

As you strive for maturity through following Christ, you will build an environment of trust by being open and fully exposed, which aids in creating an intimate and harmonious setting. If a marriage can create the kind of intimacy within itself that is true and holy, that kind of marriage can be utilized by God and will give Him the adoration He desires—a marriage of oneness that lifts up a true worship!

CHAPTER SEVEN

MAN'S POSITION OF AUTHORITY IN COMMUNITY/WORLD

From the beginning, the purpose of mankind's creation was not only to reverence God the Father but also to create harmonious relationships. Created in His image, man was formed from greatness—and promised that if he lived in the *light*, he would not only dwell in a glorious city, but would be the light of the world (Matthew 5:14, 16).

As God has demonstrated throughout history, when man follows the commands and lives his life according to holiness, all the things of the earth placed under his authority falls in place (his existence, marriage/relationships, his abilities, government and the earth/environment). God's promises will not return to Him void. The Scripture states, *"God is not a man, that He should lie..."* (Numbers 23:19), and those promises, which declare benefits to His truth, still exist today, if only man will *"...Obey my voice, and I will be your God..."* (Jeremiah 7:23). God will not deny man anything that he should ask, think or desire, within His permissive will. When man humbly follows God's ways, his relationships, possessions or circumstances are all destined to spiritually align themselves for the good because man has responded to God (the Word). Since the entrance of sin at the Fall, it has been difficult to visualize how such a spiritual and harmonious relationship existed between man and God. But it did, and it can exist again. Our God wants that relationship restored through the yearning and love man first had for Him; therefore, He sent His *Son* to be an example of that perfect relationship. Like Jesus, we are all inherently God's children (even the disobedient ones), but man must believe and recognize God first in his life.

Surrendering your life is the first step toward growing faith, readying yourself for a planned work already destined for you. Allow Jesus Christ's example to show that *way*, that *truth*, and that *life*! Only then can God's guidance move man again in the direction of a spiritual relationship with Him while he also learns to build man's natural relationships with each other!

The Bible shows us that human relationships are created through many different connections (e.g., marriages, friendships, business partnerships, etc.), but these are only sustained through demonstrations where friendliness and a sincere heart offers God's love to others. This certainly should be an evident practiced in our homes, but also evidence when we build good relationships in our communities and neighboring countries.

Throughout the ages, mankind began to meld and establish different lifestyles, clearly seen in the diversity of people, various cultural backgrounds and countless residential dwellings. All make up different communities composed of cities, boroughs, districts, suburbs, and metropolitan areas, and in some countries, even villages/tribes. These various communities of wonderful people, languages and cultures around the globe, shape and arrange our world. However, although man lives in diverse places, no one escapes God's universal or eternal truths, which are excellent and divine. They apply to every person on the face of the earth. People everywhere are evidence of His undeniable truth that all share the same human design, characteristics, potentials, and social abilities. These human traits exist for everyone—especially when it comes to the characteristic of man's loving one another!

Love is a natural emotion fashioned in such a way that it causes us to yearn it from others. Beginning at infancy, whether through touch, communication, physical closeness, or sight—love is a gift that instinctively connects. God's purpose and plan was that man would connect to each other by means of love, the very tool needed to position him back to spiritual works. These works would be purposefully designed for functioning through and with others for His good pleasure. Man was never meant to be in this world alone without the love found in human relationships. It's a truth that's proven from the very beginning when God thought it not good for man to be alone, and He created Eve for Adam (cf. Genesis 2:18; 1 Corinthians 11:9). Man would cease to exist without some type of human contact. Whether ceasing affected his spirit, mind, or body, the wholeness of man would diminish.

Relationships are generally expected to be a friendly and respectful connection. However, good relationships are dwelling places that build joy, trust, comfort and security; while others are valued to be embraced like family. Our God and Heavenly Father remind us to fix our minds on this very idea. He gives us these two very important commandments found in Matthew 22:37-39, which says:

> *"Jesus said unto him, Thou shalt love the Lord thy God with all thy heart, and with all thy soul, and with all thy mind. *[38]*This is the first and great commandment. *[39]*And the second is like unto it, Thou shalt love thy neighbour as thyself."*

Do you often examine yourself to see how you really love your Lord and Savior? Is your love superficial or a genuine love? Can you really say you love God and not love a family member or your neighbor? He says, *"If a man say, I love God, and hateth his brother, he is a liar; for he that loveth not his brother whom he hath seen, how can he love God whom he hath not seen?"* (1 John 4:20).

A daily self-examination before God is imperative for man to remain humble and honest. Can you truthfully answer this question: "How do I really love God, my fellow man, and myself?" Do you have a spiritual relationship with God where you follow His commandments? Or is that relationship lacking and causing other relationships to suffer because you lack the trust and authority of God? Do you act out of a godly character that moves you to righteousness, or do you act out of selfishness? Are your motives about gaining and not building? Failing to connect with God will cause man's destruction and doom his relationships. If your actions are truly ungodly, a very real, but frightening, character exists. Principalities with power exist in this earthly realm. Their power comes from the Adversary and the prince of this world wanting the opposite of what God instituted for relationships. Ungodly forces and evil attributes within man can surface in the presence of good—even to the point of disgracing that which God has instituted—in not rendering respect, dignity and honor where it is due (cf. Mark 12:17; Romans 13:7).

It is a detriment to man to harbor hatred in his heart for another when he professes to love God. To say that you hate someone really says that you hate God, who created the "someone" you hate, along with all of the other things of this earth. Aside from pigmentation, is every man so different that it would cause him the inability to relate to another human being? Our speech is not the only behavior that spews hatred (and certainly words do enough damage), but our hateful attitudes and actions can destroy to a whole new level! Who informed one group that they were superior and another inferior? Judging is God's position; man is not to judge another outside of righteous judgment—where a man's principles are called to live the example of Christ. Hatred is a learned or mimicked behavior viewed and followed as early as childhood. Yet, in spite of these actions, man's exposure to life should lead him to understand right and wrong—mimicking such behaviors can no longer be excused as ignorance; rather as making a deliberate choice.

Don't allow the Enemy to cause you to lose confidence when making the right choices. God is always there to keep your foot planted in the right direction, preventing your exposure (cf. Proverbs 3:26). He is the Source for all direction if man will ask and be confident in Him (cf. 1 John 5:14). However, the opposite is also true. When man lacks confidence, outside influences can make an indelible impact—molding character that could easily create *fixed* behaviors—and when a man look to others to build his confidence, the character and image is altered, thus becoming fake and out of sorts. Lacking confidence constantly causes one to feel they must prove or impress—even if it means being condescending to others. Every person was created to receive the same respect; it's a position that acknowledges that you "see" the individual as yourself—the gift of human dignity. It is man's responsibility to be kind to all by learning how to apply God's love in every life. When embracing a life of love that inhabits positive influences and appealing behaviors, all citizens become the benefactors.

Unfortunately, some areas of challenged behavior have long gone unchecked or just unawares. Sometimes behaviors have been practiced so long that they become common, and the errors cannot be seen. They are areas in behaviors that have become man's norm and must be corrected with the help of those around him. At such times, true friendships are treasures. For one to hear truth lovingly from a trusted friend, even when it hurts, is invaluable. In any confrontation or difficult situation, love causes us to care for the other. In wisdom, we conform to using pleasant words to ease tension. *"Pleasant words are as a honeycomb, sweet to the soul, and health to the bones"* (Proverbs 16:24). When we can genuinely love, we take care to always unveil truth to anyone, for truth's revelations are invaluable *in* growing any individual's life!

It is difficult to imagine that people who embraces unruliness, has a total disregard for others, or behaves badly are actions derived from possessing (if not an illness) a rebellious spirit. But rest assured that the Scripture says the prince of this world is Satan. He is the prince of all unruliness, and his spirit can be invited when man simply chooses to be open to ungodliness. Man either possesses God's Spirit or he possesses Satan's. The choice is yours! The very character that you display to others clearly demonstrates which choice you have made.

God has no preference or favorites with whom He loves, and He has shown this fondness through grace and mercy toward man, but God also desires man's love in return. This is the position where man reveres

God and takes His commandments to heart. Where he lives through love—which is how believers best represent God to the world. Be open to simply live a Spirit-filled life! Respecting others is honorable. Respect accepts God's perfect decision for creating every human life, accepting every distinguished character and acknowledging that everyone who exists is meant to be here.

Love helps us not to focus on irrelevant differences such as race. (There are unique differences even within a race.) More important focuses should be: are we fervent in examining our conviction in God? Are we living in His truth? These are the areas where we should be alike! Our society and religions have caused us to become judgmental and divisive, however, we need not look far to righteously judge, for this judgment starts with self! God clearly does not want His believers/ church divided, but unified—the only way His truth can serve and be manifested (Romans 16:17)!

God's Way of Becoming a Good Neighbor

Despite the biblical commands that God has already given, today mankind often adopts different ideals and values that fit individual lifestyles. Innate and especially spiritual principles for living are ignored or perhaps unawares. God's plan was to establish man in a realm of life with no divided lifestyle—holiness. There man could build a character that embraced a love for others that evil could not penetrate. Yet, as we've witnessed over the ages, man has gradually adopted a lifestyle that does not consider God or his neighbor, which supports his spiritual blindness and the undiscerning spirit that he experiences today. Somehow his independent life is now more important than the lives for whom he was created to share. Without love and care for others, this thinking breeds a self-centeredness that renders an isolated view—especially during times when it's important to exercise authority to assess or govern others fairly.

Sin blinds the thought that holiness can ever apply to man—it causes him to welcome new traditions that satisfy the flesh and not God's principles for community. These traditions steer man in directions that bypass the image of his creation (garden of Eden experience). They suppress thoughts from imagining the destinies of God's plan—the thoughts surrounding man connecting to one another for the greater work. It's the assurance within that leads to building a holy people, which creates upright citizens for community and the earth. Love, friendships, compassions, responsibility and care are all virtues hidden because God's principles are ignored. Good neighbors acknowledge and accept whoever man is in the world, are here a purpose and a segment of God's larger plan. The work is plentiful throughout the universe and the anguishes existing in our world's communities display that very idea. No matter where man resides, he was born to serve the one true God for His true work and purpose—to work in *His fields* (spreading His Truth) and building *His Kingdom* (growing believers). Man's relationship with God guides him to seek that truth for his part in this purpose and destiny for communities.

The Holy Spirit within helps to recognize that submission to God is one of the first steps to guidance. However, if your choice is not to observe God's ruling, at least don't create a stumbling block when others have submitted—respect it. But again recognizing and having respect is often where the spiritual discernment breaks down, and man begins to experience problems. These problems point to the sinful nature of man that can possess selfishness, judgment, insecurity, and hierarchal status toward one another. Desiring what is not yours to possess and other weakening characteristics that deteriorate and hinder the ability to build good relationships. They are God's reason for creating the following commandments (aside from the original ten), which must be the approach to igniting good relationships and realizing that every member of mankind is our neighbor.

Some of these examples applied to Old Testament lifestyles, but as the Scriptures of David have described from his life experiences, "*...there* *is no new thing under the sun"* (Ecclesiates 1:9). The life principles of God's thoughts toward man's living a loving, harmonious and successful life still applies to our societies today—they apply to people! Following God's principles for harmonious living means respecting and considering one another's emotions and how we leave someone feeling or embracing us. Consider these verses and God's thoughts towards man's harmonious living:

> *"Thou shalt not bear false witness against thy neighbour"* (Exodus 20:16).

> *"Thou shalt not covet thy neighbour's house, thou shalt not covet thy neighbour's wife, nor his manservant, nor his maidservant, nor his ox, nor his ass, nor any thing that is thy neighbour's"* (Exodus 20:17).

> *"Ye shall do no unrighteousness in judgment: thou shalt not respect the person of the poor, nor honor the person of the mighty: but in righteousness shalt thou judge thy neighbour.* ¹⁶*Thou shalt not go up and down as talebearer among thy people: neither shalt thou stand against the blood of thy neighbour: I am the LORD.* ¹⁷*Thou shalt not hate thy brother in thine heart: thou shalt in any wise rebuke thy neighbour, and not suffer sin upon him.* ¹⁸*Thou shalt not avenge, nor bear any grudge against the children of thy people, but thou shalt love thy neighbour as thyself: I am the LORD"* (Leviticus 19:15-18).

> *"He that backbiteth not with his tongue, nor doeth evil to his neighbour, nor taketh up a reproach against his neighbour"* (Psalm 15:3).

> *"Woe unto him that buildeth his house by unrighteousness, and his chambers by wrong; that useth his neighbour's service without wages, and giveth him not for his work"* (Jeremiah 22:13).

"Woe unto him that giveth his neighbour drink, that puttest thy bottle to him, and makest him drunken also, that thou mayest look on their nakedness!" (Habakkuk 2:15).

God has called all of us to recognize and respect our neighbors from the perspective of His love. Gaining a man's friendship is becoming neighborly and, through His commands, God has supplied a spiritual pathway that purposefully guides us to become that good neighbor. Much like our natural father would know our character, our Heavenly Father best knows his children's character, and His decrees for living are direct reminders of what is needed in man's character to connect to others. The mind must be transformed to allow the flow of good deeds, friendly conversations, and an inward power to express honesty and truth through divine love.

Love is the choice that prepares the heart and mind to interact well; it will always give respect to the treatment of our neighbors. Consider the following Scriptures:

> *"These are the things that ye shall do; Speak ye every man the truth to his neighbour; execute the judgment of truth and peace in your gates: [17]And let none of you imagine evil in your hearts against his neighbour; and love no false oath: for all these are things that I hate, saith the* LORD*"* (Zechariah 8:16, 17).

> *"Say not unto thy neighbour, Go, and come again, and tomorrow I will give; when thou hast it by thee"* (Proverbs 3:28).

> *"Let every one of us please his neighbour for his good to edification"* (Romans 15:2).

> *"Love worketh no ill to his neighbour: therefore love is the fulfilling of the law"* (Romans 13:10).

Whom should we love? All mankind deserves our love because God has no preferences! God has said in Romans 13:8, *"Owe no man any thing, but to love one another; for he that loveth another hath fulfilled the law."* When you are indebted to someone, be responsible to settle the matter promptly and righteously; also it is honorable to keep yourself in right standing with all mankind because God says what man does *owe* everyone is his *love*. Every man, woman, and child is our neighbor in every community, state, and nation; His boundary has no end. But to love God, we must become lovers of His Law. Adhering to the commandments brings Him pleasure, and following them as He has decreed carries great promises of long life and peace (cf. Proverbs 3:1, 2; Psalm 119:165). If the commandments are imprinted on the heart of man, it becomes a natural practice of what God wants instilled and exercised daily. Naturally, we can see that anyone's extending love to aid another fellow human is building a good relationship. When biblical principles are practiced and good acts are modeled, the heart is filled with joy. When biblical principles are practiced long enough, they will become natural human behaviors.

Unfortunately, many relationships have been strained. Through the ages and because of the covetous soul of man, Satan has penetrated thoughts with greed, status, pride, selfishness, and many other deficiencies that poison the character. God has already gifted man with His image, calling him to be directed for a higher and more divine work—not the kind of work that presses to advance for status, recognition or the filling of seemingly bottomless pockets. The call is for a work that fills and satisfies the heart. This work has a passion to please others without any regard for self, and a pure heart that drives one to satisfy a good deed for another in fulfilling ways.

Even though our God has created and molded each human body the same, society has infused self-centeredness and continues to mold the mind. Society offers man rewards through the appearance of success—his "winning" or elevating himself over others through a conquest for the title, prevailing and standing out from the crowd, etc., but who really wins when the goal is selfishly motivated? Love for others should raise these questions:

+ How did I win?
+ What was the outcome of the win?
+ Can I expect to rally the support of others?
+ What did I gain?

When selfishness is the premise, it certainly closes the thinking surrounding anything or anyone beyond you; after all, this image is in direct conflict with the character of God. Even religion suffers because man is divided on the one thought that mankind should innately know—there is but one Lord, one faith, and one baptism. There is no drawing any closer to God by positioning one over another. Titles come and go, but as followers of Christ, can we really say that we deserve to be entitled as Christ's *brother* or *sister*? For this reason, not all competitions or advancements good— especially when someone is made to feel *diminutive* in stature.

As I see it, the only healthy competition is that extra effort which forces us do better within ourselves. It is the drive or push that helps us to finish the race. It is the encourager when we need a pick-me-up. It is the focus needed to stay the path. But largely, it is the constant examination and desire to improve the characteristics of man and mature in the ways of holiness.

During my high school years, I had a very stern, but wise, principal. At certain times, he would request that we sing a particular song when we gathered in the auditorium for an assembly. Yes, we always sang our regular school song, but as I think back, I believe he wanted us to meditate on this song and allow the words to stir our very soul. The song was adapted from a poem by John Donne, a poet, a priest, and a lawyer who sent a strong message of the kind of mind God created in all mankind. Singing this song strengthened our attitude toward one another, permeating our soul and causing us to remember its words and embrace unification at our school. My principal's plan must have worked because the song remains in me! Donne wrote:

No man is an island,
No man stands alone.
Each man's joy is joy to me,
Each man's grief is my own.
We need one another,
So I will defend,
Each man as my brother,
Each man as my friend.
I saw the people gather,
I heard the music start,
The song that they were singing,
Is ringing in my heart.
No man is an island,
Way out in the blue,
We all look to the one above,
For our strength to renew.
When I help my brother,
Then I know that I,
Plant the seed of friendship,
That will never die.

Each of these stanzas is scriptural and depicts an image of God and a character He wants each of us to possess and model. Several Scriptures reference these same ideas and principles: "Each man's grief is my own" (cf. Romans 12:15). "We need one another" (cf. Ecclesiastes 4:9-12). "Plant the seed of friendship" (cf. Proverbs 18:24; John 15:15). As you can see, John Donne's meditative writings expressed so much of God's spiritual light and truth.

If we stepped back and viewed various truths surrounding human relationships, we would see many areas on which we could improve in our interactions. For example, in a partnership or a working relationship, many lack the ability to give praise or credit beyond themselves. In most success stories, very rarely is every part of the success brought to light. In fact, in most instances, the claim is that one person accomplished it "all on his own." God has always equipped others with skills and talents to help us along the way. Whether it is through administration, someone's funding, the suppliers, the postal/freight system, or a phone call of encouragement, *others* are always involved who have worked to help accomplish a certain goal. And whatever is believed, the truth is that God's purposes and timing cause everything to work together for its completion. Whether part of this path or journey was designed for you or someone else, God orchestrated it to happen for that time, place, and purpose. Instead of using abilities to encourage or build up one another, we get jealous and tend to demean, undermine, or deceive for the sake of getting ahead and gaining status or titles.

Love embraces others' successes (...*each man's joy is joy to me..*); love embraces others at a level of acceptance without becoming judgmental. Love is like a blanket that, when spread out and shared, demonstrates that all mankind are really at the same level when seated at God's feet.

Our God is the wonderful God of this universe, and He has imagined a wonderful, beneficial way of life for every person through His truth. Living in Him and being guided by His light offers truth that our spirits cannot deny. His way of life is filled with promises for the present and a blessed hope for the eternal.

Knowing that life on earth is temporary, strive to be transformed to Christ-likeness and build righteous relationships for your eternal home. Whatever has to be accomplished during your time here, ask for God's help in faith and then believe. Stand firm and allow Him to open the door. There is nothing that cannot be accomplished if it's in His will. Submit to His commands, and you will live and operate all things through love.

Those who choose to seek and follow Christ's way of life know that there is a purpose for this love. Reaching out to others in our communities and beyond is the example that Jesus left for us to emulate. A perfect example was demonstrated when He instructed His disciples to go and teach His message. He did not ask them to stay in their hometown or region; rather, He said, "...go ye...and teach all nations..." (Matthew 28:19). Christ issued a message to go beyond the comforts of man's familiarity to preach love and truth to all nations for all times. His message is to be shared liberally with no requirements, obligations, or boundaries. No one in the world is to be denied access or to be excluded from His truth and love.

Who Is My Neighbor? Who Is a Friend?

A lawyer once posed a question to Jesus in Scripture: "Who is my neighbor?" Jesus answered by telling him the parable of the good Samaritan (cf. Luke 10:25-37). There were three different men who traveled on a road. On separate occasions, two different travelers crossed to the other side of this road to avoid a man who had been beaten and robbed, stripped of his clothes, and left for dead. But when the third traveler saw him, he had compassion and took it upon himself to attend to the man's wounds and his immediate needs, placing him under the assistance of a local innkeeper, and promising to return to pay for any added cost for the man's care.

When Jesus asked the man posing the question, "Of these three, who was the neighbor?" the man answered, *"He that showed mercy on him."* Then Jesus answered and said, *"...Go, and do thou likewise"*(John 10:37).

We are all one another's neighbors. God's dream for mankind goes far beyond any one individual. His dream may extend beyond what is comfortable for our loving others enough to see a need, denying ourselves sacrificially, becoming an encourager, having compassion with empathy, and simply doing for others as we would want them to do for us. Jesus has said, *"Go, and do thou likewise."* Can you imagine what Jesus meant by these words? His command is a mission in itself, and if it were realized, we would see that these acts would create the same atmosphere of "His will being done in earth as it is in heaven!"

Our neighbors are not simply those living next door or across the street, but they are also those who can be reached in the far regions of Africa, Europe, Asia, North America, and beyond. God has people all over the universe to whom we can extend our love and helping hands. As inhabitants of this earth, God wants us to live lovingly among our close neighbors—but to be spiritually heightened is to recognize Him, and to see *"thyself"* in all societies. Only then will we understand the passage in His Word, *"For all the law is fulfilled in one word, even in this; Thou shalt love thy neighbour as thyself"* (Galatians 5:14). A genuine neighbor cares that every person is fed, clothed, housed, and has work. The person who lives by this commandment will understand that the elderly who poured their life into others, must be cared for in their twilight years with honor. Following the admonition of Galatians 5:14 will benefit all men's souls to rest in contentment—knowing they have fulfilled God's call for the spiritual wealth of man. He has created this character in all man to embrace one another—a power that possesses hearts to genuinely *love*.

Is God Your Friend, Your "First Love"?

As a man that God created, how do you express your love for Him? Do you live by God's Word or by your own standards or code? Are you the one who created yourself, the earth, an environment or established the laws for government? Do you acknowledge and reverence a God who demonstrates with blaring evidence and wonders that He is alive, holy and has given His Son as example of the way, the truth and the life?

These are the type of questions that man should consider—even through self-examination! Be honest and ask yourself the following questions: "Am I spiritually blind?" "Am I a man who truly loves my

Heavenly Father? If I say I love Him, do I live to please Him?" Not recognizing and living a life outside of the Father's guidance is not love and does not bring Him glory. God wants to mature Spirit-filled men who reflect His character in this world. Allow God's Word to mature you and to enhance your spiritual understanding causing fear to dissipate— then stand to display the true inner strength of God through humility. Don't allow *pride* to destroy any possibility of seeing or acknowledging God and His many blessings—not having humility will prevent your recognizing God, therefore, the gains of life will be attributed to your credit—never giving God glory. Taking this position is dangerous and a constant detriment to the image God created in you—a holy character. Don't give up; ask for God's guidance and press toward being that holy and upright man.

God's grace is offered new every morning, and man is still allowed *today* to alter his thinking and accept His Heavenly Father's ways. Man must make the choice to return His devotion and to make God his "first love" again. This means respecting God in every part of life. Become grateful for God's grace and revere Him daily through—prayer, worship, relationships, direction, conversation, work, outreach, and especially for his destined purpose.

Know that your being on this earth has purpose—seek it! As small as you may seem to be in this grand universe, God's plan and need of you was already designed before your birth. You were born with an innate gift that is revealed through a relationship with your Father. Some recognize it early in life, while others will need to be guided to see it. Either way it takes a relationship with the Father to guide you in how to make use of it. Every day that your gift is not utilized is a day or an opportunity lost where someone could have benefited from your impartation. Mature in God and share to better someone else's life. This mission is bigger than any single person; it is universal and meant to establish a love that stretches far and wide and establishes a premise of equality in mankind across the globe.

The prince of this world and his demons win when they can remind you of your past or your sin nature to the point that it paralyzes you to do nothing! His tool of defeat is to inflict doubt, prompting questions like, "Who am I that God should chose me?" "What can I do?" "What skills do I possess?" Know the Word that has been given to you. *"Ye are of God, little children, and have overcome them: because greater is he that is in you, than he that is in the world"* (1 John 4:4). Know yourself through your Father's love. Walk boldly in Him and act in the godly authority that has been given to you. Much work is yet to be done in His field [the world], and holy men are needed to take their righteous position. Take up your Christian arms, pray without ceasing, and stand in His power. Remember that love conquers all. Know without a doubt that God loves you because He created you for Himself. Above all, love God and allow his light to shine in you for the world—and Love is the brightest!

PRAYER FOR LOVE AND RESTORATION

Jehovah God of scripture, Heavenly Father and Friend,

I want to thank you for the love shown in creating my life, and the grace that you've extended me throughout the years. Thank you for all you've allowed my hands to possess and my mind to understand. Forgive me for not recognizing the abilities and treasures that I've acquired are gifts from you—for they were given for your purpose. Now give me the wisdom to use them for your glory. Help me to build a relationship with you, filling me with your Holy Spirit—empower me through your guidance to rule and govern in this dominion with righteous authority. Open my spiritual understanding to know when I'm at odds with my brother, not to hate him but to spiritually discern who's behind every evil action. Help me to learn how to equip myself with the whole armour of your spiritual defense to war against our adversary. Sin has caused generations to become blind to your original thoughts for mankind—but especially towards man who was showered with your love supremely for a priestly position. Help me to view that position of priesthood predestined for me. Allow my heart to be taught again your love and your ways— and the purposes for me in your plan. Knowing now that with love and my submission to your commands, all things in this dominion (family, work, relationships, and spiritual understanding) will all fall into place, through your permissive will, for the purposes of building that hope—a life in your Eternal Kingdom. I ask this prayer in the name of your Son, Jesus Christ—Amen!

ACKNOWLEDGEMENT

I'd first like to thank my God and King for this opportunity to write "It's Time"—the journey and truths regarding men of a Holy priesthood.

Where God began this impetus journey of seeking and writing these pages over a decade ago, I can't say that it's always been easy, comfortable or even adequate when attempting to express many of these topics. But through God's guidance it's been His love that's given me the strength and sufficient abilities to speak His truths in Love.

My thanks go out to so many who were on this journey with me these many years. First to God for guiding every turn that needed exploring. To my husband who patiently prayed and allowed me time to write this book. To my mother who always encouraged me to teach and my siblings who were held captives as kids for my story telling and performances. To a career that offered teaching opportunities through its infrastructure, writing for my sister's (Chaplain Arquilla Conner-Dabney) Pen Pal prison ministry, to the unveiling bible studies of Bishop Garrison. Also, remembering a host of family and elders who were examples in holding up the name of Jesus before a young child.

Finally, for Westbow Press and Gwen Ash's professional assistance and enthusiasm—their team of editors who guided a novice with ways to express my voice. Additionally, to dear ones like Doris Haulcy, Celeste Sharper-Wooten, and Linda Stubblefield; instrumental in reading and offering feedback of the book's contents, thank you—your prayers, love, encouragement, and sometimes thrust, helped to remind me to trust

God and to see the importance of completing this journey—thank you Father for each of them!

And especially to all my family and friends who continue to offer their love by sharing this wonderful life we live through Christ Jesus.

NOTES

NOTES

NOTES

NOTES

NOTES

NOTES

NOTES

NOTES

NOTES

NOTES

NOTES

NOTES

NOTES

NOTES

NOTES

Printed in the United States
By Bookmasters